The Diary Of A Misfit

The Diary Of A Misfit

A Memoir

By
Palesa Lepheana

Classic Age
PUBLISHING

ISBN 13 : 978-0-9947069-8-0

Classic Age
PUBLISHING

Published by in 2017 by

Po Box 134, Braamfontein, South Africa, 2001.

Printed and bound by Digital Action, Cape Town, South Africa.

Proofread by Vukulu Sizwe Maphindani

Typesetting by Rosa Penn

Cover Design by Exadesign
Website : www.classicagepublishing.co.za
Email : info@classicagepublishing.co.za

Welcome to Hell

I HAD TO leave my luggage in the dining hall; I didn't study my surroundings or look at everyone or the dining hall in particular; I was overpowered by my anger and had to exit the room at once. I stood outside while my uncle took the rest of my belongings inside. I wasn't interested in anything; all I did was to gaze in the sky that had few altostratus clouds. I hoped and prayed that God or Jesus will appear from them riding a white unicorn to save me from the torture that was ahead of me. Far away from the village, were a huge and scary, scary looking mountains that looked like they were going to collapse anytime and bury the whole village together with the school beneath the earth surface. The mountains were petrifying and I even imagined a huge creature appearing behind them, I was definitely sure that there was something huge behind them that no one knew about. I thought I was going to some school back home in Matatiele. My interview was unsuccessful; thanks to me and my clumsiness in my head that had shoe-glue all over, but that's a story for another day.

"Palesa come in so the ladies can see you" my uncle Tshepang woke me from my daydream. I then followed him inside to where I was introduced to Ausi Mathapelo, they called her "mama" she was the one who looked after the girls and locked them in whenever it is time to sleep or wake up; check sleep outs and the girls' rooms whether they were clean or not. Ausi Mathapelo was about 5.7m tall; chocolate in complexion, body average, and she had beautifully arranged white teeth in her mouth; though I thought her laugh was loud and irritating. She was also one of the ladies that cooked for us, quite obvious she couldn't just look after the girls and do nothing while they were at school, it made sense, she would die out of loneliness and boredom.

We were done with everything including paying for accommodation; I was told that I was going to get a room later on. I wasn't interested in everything that was happening that day; all I thought about was my life, it was over finished! I know a lot of teens get excited about being sent to boarding school, just for the sake of freedom; but I wasn't, freedom was the last thing on my mind, I didn't want any of that. What was I going to do with it anyway? I haven't been to parties and mostly no boyfriend, it was final that I was going to marry myself "for richer for poor." My uncle introduced me to two boys that he knew from back home, Tshepang and Toka. I thought I've seen them somewhere though I was young and stupid. I couldn't remember where I had seen them. They promised to look after me and save my poor soul from all the bad things ahead, I was shocked and had to confirm from my uncle once more,"did he just ask a bunch of silly looking boys to look after me?" I thought to myself. I studied them from top to bottom and the way they presented themselves, they were up to no good and one of them looked like he was a drug addict.

I was sixteen and had never kissed a boy in my life all thanks to my uncle; I had never in my life given a boy a chance to talk to me, not even to say "hi". He really surprised me and somehow I found myself laughing and had to reply by saying ... "yeah I will look after them too". I have been preached at and shouted at; all in the name of boys!

Boys will make you pregnant; they will promise you the world they don't even have themselves.

"They will ruin your future."

"They will give you aids."

"They only want sex from you."

"They are liars."

"They were all breastfed by the same woman."

"They will pass at school and you won't."

"Once they touch you, your life is over!"

Then he said, "that is where I will come in I will beat you up much that you won't be able to walk again, you hear me?" He said. I knew he wasn't joking, my uncle would drive from Egypt to South Africa to give me a hiding if he had to; he has been like that to my mom as well, I wonder if it had ever crossed his mind that my mom was older than him.

I wasn't ready for everything that was going to happen for the next twelve months; I've seen the worst, I've seen my friends getting married at the age of twelve, 'I've seen a couple having sex in the woods at the age of ten. Trust me, when I tell you that I'm still traumatized and yes I saw a rooster sitting next to red looking boys from the mountains, literally it was following them everywhere they went even to the toilet; but I was told that the rooster died afterwards and it wasn't supposed to be eaten by anyone, black magic they say. Going to a primary school at sixteen was the worst of them all, it was more than just black magic; it was a spell from another planet sent to destroy me.

I pictured myself being the only tall girl in school; everyone was short and little. It wasn't again the first time that "d be looking older than the other kids. Years ago before I came to stay in Joburg I was staying with my grandmother's sister; I had cousins Hopolang, Tshepang, and abuti Diketso. My grandmother Manchekoane never gave up on making myself and Hopolang twins. It was her wish that we could've been twins and from the same mother, we were younger and were sent to the same daycare, even though I knew that I was a year older than Hopolang. I was the oldest, the tallest and everyone was short and little including Hopolang. The kids were scared of me and I somehow used the privilege and I always had things done my way. I understood that my granny didn't want me and Hopolang to be separated but again Hopolang was enjoying her days more than I did as I would protect her if she got into trouble. So it felt like the past was repeating itself if it wasn't coming back , it terrified me to death to even think of that, I wasn't ready to be bullied by little kids telling me how tall and ugly I was; that was the last thing I needed in my plate.

Yes, I was admitted at a primary school; I found out that Sekgutlong starts from grade ten. I left Joburg knowing that I was going to high school but things didn't go according to plan; literally, lady luck was not on my side as much as I thought she was, coming to think of high school; 'I've been to high school, back in my previous school in Joburg. I never felt left out or neither did I demonstrate that I was in grade 8 or not. What I knew was that I was in high school. New Model started from grade eight to twelve and had grade R too. I prayed they shouldn't take me and I even crossed my fingers hard enough to feel my veins paining under my skin. Unfortunately, I was admitted and I was going to start school the following day. If I had a dagger in my hands that day I would have stabbed myself and let the pain take away my misery.

Mononthsa the primary school; was less than a kilometre away from the hostel, so I had to walk there every day. The most embarrassing thing I thought was going to happen to my life. I was tall and appeared very old; if I had to lie and say I was married and had two children everyone were to take me seriously. I've reached puberty and have been on my periods for the rest of my life; my armpits had hair and it was combable, my hips were wider than those of Sarah Baartman, I didn't think I deserved to be in primary. In fact, I shouldn't have been in primary. Not even a single drop of tears fell from my chicks-I had to save that for later; it was going to be acceptable for me to cry when Uncle Tshepang left and everyone was going to understand my reasons; On top of the list was that I was neglected and didn't know where I was. I didn't know what was going to happen to me later that afternoon; maybe I will be dead the next morning. I was literally going to die out of negligence. I was certain that wherever my mom is she was tossing and turning in her grave. I made a silent prayer that Uncle Tshepang would sit down and consider the whole decision of leaving me behind but he didn't. I realized that he meant business and he was sure of leaving me behind and I had no choice but to suck it up. I needed myself more than I needed any motivation from anyone not even that of Nelson Mandela. He didn't know me and neither did he know that I was being sent to an unknown village in the middle of nowhere. So I held my head up high - though I walked like a zombie I had to go back and face those naughty kids I saw running around the hostel earlier. First I had to head straight to the kitchen that was already closed. Ausi Mathapelo was waiting for me outside with my bags on the floor.

Hostel

Carrying my bags from the dining hall to the girl's hostel was sad. It was a mission impossible. I made a reticent prayer; thanking God I wasn't given a metal trunk. Remembering that I stole my mom's small heart-shaped pillow; plus all my toiletries were stashed in the same giant suitcase altogether. Everyone was scattered outside like cockroaches. For a minute I thought I was brought to a stout school, no one volunteered to assist me with my bags. Ausi Mathapelo's hands were full. She was holding a half loaf of brown bread, a bowl that I was sure it had food as it was covered with a glass plate, two boiled eggs in a plastic and juice in a water bottle, I was scared and all I thought of were the stories I heard about boarding schools; that included"Spud", the book I read by John Van De Ruit; it was about a young boy who went to boarding school, he was given the name Spud because he had a small penis and his balls had not dropped. I knew that I was also going to get a new name like spud and it's either I was or won't be everyone's favourite. Coming to think of names, I was again grateful that I left my previous school and was forever praying that I won't be given a name too. Back in Joburg, they used to call me "Joshua Door" they used the name of a furniture shop, reason being that the logo had an old white men whose hair starts in the middle of his head and they said I had his resemblance my forehead, was terrible, I had fluffy hair with no hairline; my hair starts in the middle of my head leaving the forehead exposed. I actually didn't know whom to blame for this - my mom, dad or God. If I had to put on weaves I would have to make sure that I cover it up or get a Chinese fringe cut. So that's how I got the name but a few people knew that and I was glad that they didn't call me that as some pupils from other countries in Africa didn't have a clue as to who Joshua Door was unless they googled him.

From the main door, I was welcomed by a nauseating smell of Jeyes fluid, it was all over the passage; the hostel was huge and had more rooms than it looked from the outside. "I expect your corridor to be clean at all times" Ausi Mathapelo instructed. I paused for few seconds, what is a corridor? And why do I have such a stupid responsibility? No one was there to answer my questions as I was speaking to myself. My room was huge and empty I had to get everything I needed all by myself, that included a bed and a locker. I was told I was going to have a roommate the next day; the thought made me so nervous as if I was going to share a room with the queen of England.

I spent the rest of the afternoon in my room, unpacking, and packing. You took the whole wardrobe here palesa. I didn't have anyone to talk to but myself, maybe I was going to talk to myself for as long as I lived, well maybe that's what I thought. I heard some noise from the passage, somehow I managed to hear a very deep voice of a man that echoed through the passage together with tiny voices that sounded like chipmunks which were getting closer to my door. A tall bold headed man walked in my room, right after one or two knocks, he asked if I was ok, and he advised he came to check if I owned a curtain and had found all I needed as the hostel was out of the mattress. How can that be? Why was I admitted in the first place? of course, I didn't ask the questions, I didn't have the guts to even ask about a rat I saw running to the toilet earlier on. The rat was big and fat I even thought it was a pat and I swear it was the size of a shoe owned by Sultan Kosen the tallest man in the world.

The man introduced himself as Ntate Moloi "Papa" and he was looking after the boys and did the same job as Ausi Mathapelo, though he wasn't a cook but the school driver. Ntate Moloi was tall, light-skinned, body built. He was the kindest man I've met since my arrival; he would smile for no reason. He spoke softly like there was a sponge candy in his mouth; he was clean and dressed for his age.

The whole night I was awake and it was almost time to wake up, I thought I was going to be sick or I was already sick, I didn't know how I felt. My head was heavy and my eyes were red and sore, my tummy made a lot of funny sounds. To tell the truth I haven't been sleeping for the past four weeks since I found out that I was going to a province where I didn't have family or knew anyone. I did nothing but to stay awake and protect myself. The last thing I wanted was to wake up in the middle of nowhere. I knew and have googled about boarding schools before I arrived,

"Expect the unexpected"

"Always stay alerted and keep your eyes open"

"Anything can happen"

I had to wake up and get ready to face another day in hell. The streaks of the sun peeped through the sides of our so-called curtain that reflected from the window to my face and I had to blink once or twice to recover. Somehow we found the poor curtain abandoned in some scary dark room around the hostel. The noise on the corridor was the reason why I couldn't sleep. I couldn't believe these girls didn't sleep the whole night, I wondered what were they busy doing all night. And there was this noisy girl I think they called her Tumie, she was one of the girls who accompanied Ntate Moloi to my room last night, and she kept on smacking doors . Laughing out loud and kept saying "many were coridong" , to my surprise some girl was shouting on the corridor and kept saying "she was also new". Tumie was light in complexion, long white teeth, not perfectly shaped with a little ass that suits her body perfectly fine and actually not bad looking but I think my forehead was better than hers. Something hit me and I wondered if she had a boyfriend; she was childish, loud and irritating. I prayed she didn't have a boyfriend and I prayed she didn't have a crush either. I was pretty much sure that whoever she was crushing on was living a life of a mole,always hiding and living in a hole, impossible!

Roommate number one

Mantahli my roommate was still asleep, oh God I prayed I

didn't forget her name, she was the most beautiful thing I've ever set my eyes on, she wasn't bad at all. I would have actually complained if maybe she had a twin sister but good for her because she didn't have one. Matahli was a dark beauty, slim figure, with long legs, she had a perfect body that convinced me that Beyonce would think it would do her justice - if she had to do her famous dance moves. All I hoped and prayed for was that she would be good to me and I to her, I hoped that we would become best of friends and share almost everything, though she was slim. I didn't have a problem with clothes and wasn't planning to borrow from anyone but I felt like I wanted to share them with someone close to me and she were to be that close to me as she was my roommate. Before coming to Qwaqwa I had decided that I wanted someone who will be more than just a friend to me, it wasn't because I needed a friend but because I was going to be alone and needed someone I could trust or someone to defend me, four years was going to be a long ride and I needed someone to trust, support me and feel safe with. I had a friend back in Joburg -Sindy Mthombeni, my true best friend and yes we used to exchange clothes, I loved her so much and the idea of being away from her was going to kill me. Sindy was too beautiful to be human, she had a beautiful body; her legs were to die for mostly when she wore her red Scottish school skirt. She was amazing and if God had to send an angel for me to grant my wish I knew exactly what I wanted- just by looking at my BFF.

I met Mantahli yesterday, just after papa and those silly girls left our room, I thought I was told she was going to come the next day, she was also a newcomer I had to make sure that I welcomed her so she wouldn't think of me as a bad person, God forbid I wasn't taught to be rude in my life. I even tried to help her get a bed and we went to Papa to look for a spare mattress in Block B. I was busy looking at the things she came with and thought to myself who the hell would actually send their child to a boarding school with small bags as if they'll return tomorrow or whenever. of course that was before she told me she is from the surrounding areas in qwaqwa, then again I thought who the f$@^$%# would waste time and money to bring their kids to live here while their home is just around the corner, Mantahli answered all my silent questions as if she was reading my mind, to my surprise she told me that the school expects the pupils to be here by 7 am. Thank IGod I wasn't part of the furniture!

Our room was too large for the both of us, the floor had cheap looking white tiles, the windows were covered with fencing; it felt like a prison, our small quarter beds were far apart from each other, did II mention that the beds didn't have springs? There was no way a child was to be happy when jumping on top of them, I was more worried about my spinal cord actually the rest of my precious body was in trouble. There was a huge table that we pushed to the window I thought it was for studying if not dining, we have had two green ugly looking lockers for our clothes which I thought they were just too ugly to belong to a school, soldiers were definitely going to appreciate them than myself or any other girl in the hostel.

It was time to take a bath, I had to wait for Mantahli to

bath first as I didn't know that we had to use bowls to bath, showers weren't in a good position to be utilised, she came prepared. I had to fetch water from the toilets in order to bath, the last time I did that was back at home in matatiele. I blamed my uncle tshepang for everything I felt like he ruined my youth, he was the reason behind my frustration and that included my sorrows to follow while I was stuck in that place.

The toilets smelled terrible but thankfully I had to only fetch warm water and leave the smell behind me. The floor had no tiles but just brown rough cement that was wet and slimy under my slippers, the room consisted of five un-operational showers which looked more like taps than showers, the toilet cubicles didn't have doors and were totally exposed, I even doubted if they flushed, they looked non-operational. If a ghost came out in there I wasn't going to surprised-surely I was just going to have to apologise to the poor thing for disturbing its peace.

I was all dressed up and ready for breakfast, I found myself walking through the main door for three minutes that felt like an hour and a half, the corridor was narrow, our room was the last one at the end of all the rooms, it was room fourteen the last one next to the other entrance that looked like it has never been opened for the past 100 decades, finally I made it to the noisy girls outside, who were already eating four slices of brown bread out of their hands with their cups of cold tea-yes the tea looked cold because of no steam that was visible from the cups. The bread looked dry and some girl was peeling off the crust around the small slices and eating only the middle part of the bread, of course, the rest she was throwing away.

On the way to the dining hall on the right hand side was the middle doormat for the boys 'Block B', the buildings were similar in colour and shape, but only the stairs were built differently, the boys ones were much higher and ours were we lower with only two rows and I head they had more rooms than ours, on the left-hand side was a dining hall where there used to have tables to eat and it was now used as a school hall. Then far down was block C the other and no one was staying in there but ghosts as I was told.

The dining hall was wide and huge, it was divided into two, where we stood to queue for food; the other side were huge silver metal pots and everything the cooks needed. I wondered how the ladies cooked all the food and how they stirred the food. Inside were three ladies ausi-Mathapelo-whom I've already met, ausi-Salaminah and mme maMoloi. Ausi-Salaminah was light skinned, short and body averaged with long brown hair; at first, I thought she was coloured I even asked myself; what does a coloured lady cook for black people. Mme Moloi was also body average light skinned but not like Ausi Salaminah, she had a beautiful smile and from what I saw I thought she didn't get angry at some point, unlike the mysterious faces of Ausi Salaminah and Ausi-Mathapelo.

So it was a norm to take food with no plates but your hands, "what manners" I thought to myself. I followed the norm and did what others did. After all, I didn't want others to think I was a drama queen, or just like that girl from legally blonde the movie. On our way back the boys were sitting on the stairs eating their bread and some didn't have cups and used tumblers and half cut water bottles to drink their tea. Somehow I found myself laughing and asking myself why my uncle brought me here. And was I that crazy and corrupt to be brought to a crazy school like this with all these weird creatures.

Mantahli and I joined the other girls outside to finish eating before they can head to school, we heard a very disturbing noise made by the boys from block B, they were screaming and laughing at some boy who looked like he just woke up and was rushing to the dining hall while it was already closed."The poor soul, he won't eat for the next four hours until break time" I thought to myself.

"Ditebogo is always late for everything," said the other light skinned girl with the horse voice. She laughed so hard that I managed to see the ending of her tongue down her throat. She was very pretty and had beautiful everything I thought she was perfect, God literally gave her everything and made sure she was beautifully created. She was light skinned and at some point, I noticed that her seSotho accent sounded different from the others. I didn't want to be forward and ask where she came from.

I headed back to my room to get ready for school, to my surprise I saw the other girls who were still not dressed and some were still naked and not yet ready to go to school. The time was 6:50 and I realised that it was unfair to wake up early so to make it to the dining hall for dry bread and cold tea that was called breakfast while school started at 7 am. I truly understood the pressure the girls were under, after all, ladies will always be ladies, we have the right to our beauty sleep and time for our faces before we can kick starts our day.

"Banana ntate Kgoabane ke eo" a girl screaming from the main door meaning 'girls. Mr Kgoabane is coming' everyone lost their minds, screaming and slamming the doors, some still naked, while others were running with their heavy backpacks to the main door. I found myself running as well, I didn't know who he was, what he does but I what I realised was that he's not a man to mess with!

A tall, bold headed man walked straight to the main door caring a cane, wearing a light green shirt, grey striped tie, grey pants and a brown jacket with black and shiny shoes, he was whipping everyone everywhere, he didn't care where he was whipping them, all the girls were scattered everywhere outside screaming and laughing at him."Nthabiseng come here" he said to one of the girls we were having tea with earlier on. I also thought she was cute and her dreadlocks made her stand out of the crowd.

I was standing still at my door, frozen, he was heading my direction "hey you come here, can't you see its time for school? Why are you standing there and why are you not dressed for school?" he questioned. I was frozen and didn't know how to reply. I mean the thing is according to the rules 'no man was allowed to enter our dormitories' but he just did and he even came straight to my room. "Um...I..." I stuttered. He was holding my hand, waiting for me to surrender so I can get a lash. I was speechless as I was not part of the school but only for the boarding. I had my uncle Tshepang to blame for that too, it was his fault.

"No! No! Mr K she's not part of the school" a loud and roughly voice came from the main door, she's heading towards us, coming to rescue me from the angry man. "She's in primary Mr. K" miss rough voice said. She's so beautiful with a voice that's not hers, wearing a kaki dickies pants, kaki dickies shirt and black and polished toughies shoes. Somehow I think this is gangsterism or strange for a girl so ...so beautiful. "No...No...I am not part of this school sir" I said.i rolling my eyes at him with anger and confusion. How can he attempt to kill an innocent girl like me?

I didn't blame Mr K, I was old at tooth; I was more of a fossil than being in the primary. If only there was a way out, I was willing to do it. I stood there frozen, wishing that I was in movies. I also wished to be Cinderella and had a Godmother; I knew if I had to make a wish, it was going to be granted. All I needed was to be patient, study to pass so I can come here and be part of the furniture.

"Study hard, pass then come to Sekgutlo" that was my motto.

Monontsha Primary school

Everyone was already gone thanks to Mr K, the hostel was now quiet and I was waiting for my time too so I could hit the sack. What warmed my heart the most was the fact that I wasn't going to school alone; there was a girl in a lower class I think in grade 8 if I am not mistaken. Slender is what they called her and I was also expected to call her that too, even though I felt bad and shy to call a plump person by that name, slender was a very big girl for her age, she was light skinned in colour, 6m tall, she had the most beautiful smile and her chicks would get much bigger if she was forced to laugh.

"Who is that," I asked Slender. I was asking about an old man who was busy cutting the grass just before the main school gate. She told me its Ntate Matangtang, he was the school gardener and we were to see him every day. I thought he was just too old to work, just after we passed the classes, Slender showed me his house. The house was inside of the school yard, it was painted the same colour as the sekgutlong uniform and classes. She told me the school had given the house to him and his also staying there with his family. She told me that Ntate Matang-tang is the one who locks and unlocks all the classes. Coming to think of the classes, I thought they were just too many of them to handle all by him.

On our way to school, we came across a swarm of bees and we had to run and stop, they were behind us. Poor slender had to run and I couldn't wait for her because I'd be risking my life to be strung by one of the bees. I was still thinking why in the hell we had to be so unlucky and be chased by bees, it then crossed my mind that we were wearing yellow or gold shirts as part of our uniform and the worst part was that we were stuck with the shirts for the next twelve months. I don't know about slender her life was only going to get worse; she still had two to three years to go.

The school was clean and neat compared to where I came from, Slender and I discovered a small gate between the school and the stadium, the gate was going to save us a lot of time and no one would see if we were going to be late as we would come behind classes. I had to go see the principal so she could show me around and introduce me to one of the teachers, so much trouble the poor woman had to go through for me, but I loved the idea anyway. I had to part ways with Slender and again she's been there since the schools opened; with me and I was a month if not a few weeks late due to lying to myself that I was going to Matatiele.

The school principal had an Eccentric personality, she was an old woman, sure in her early fifties if I'm right. Mme Motaung; she had grey hair, about 4m tall if not 5m, she was wearing a beautiful brown scotch skirt with a matching diced jersey and looked very beautiful and respectful for her age. She asked if I knew how to sing and I said yes. She also asked why I wanted to come to Qwa-qwa. I had, to be honest as it wasn't my plan but a nightmare that came with my granny. "oh Mr Mokoena this is Palesa she just came in yesterday and will be in grade 9" she told the old bold headed man who walked into her office. I couldn't understand the story behind all these old bold headed gentlemen I kept on running into, I was told that qwaqwa was a very cold place to be at if I were them I was to keep my hair and let it grow just to be on the safe side.

His name was Mr Mokoena, he used his hand when he talked, and he was wearing brown brand wood trousers, brown formal shoes, and a matching diced half jersey with a green shirt. "What is the story about diced jerseys? Are they that fashionable?" I asked myself. Mr Mokoena was a neat old man and very kind too, from what I observed at that particular moment. "Hello my dear," he said. "Good morning Mr Mokoena, I am Palesa Lepheana, from Sekgutlong Hostel" I introduced myself and made sure I gave all the information he didn't ask for just to save time. "Mme Motaung, I'll take this one to my class, she will fit in perfectly fine," he said. Fit in perfectly fine? Does he have a class full of baby mamas and daddies? Or maybe tall and old looking sacks as I was?

Mr Mokoena's class consisted of 24 pupils if I am not mistaken and I was going to be the 25th, "Welcome to 9c Miss Lepheana" he said. "Thank you sir I feel welcomed already" I automatically replied. I really did feel welcomed, the class was very clean and the pupils looked amazing and well organised. They were all wearing gold shirts, gold and blue striped ties with navy blue trousers for the boys and blue skirts for the girls. Mr Mokoena asked who wanted me in their group, the whole class raised their hands and I was forced to choose where to sit, the pupils were sitting in groups facing each other. I chose the group in the middle that had two girls, Dimpho and Molelekeng. The boys were Abel, Thabang, Paseka and Thato. Before i even decided to pick a seat, I had to look around and find something to calm me down, and that was, of course, someone who looked older than I was. I smiled a little and my breathing picked up and my heart was beating faster than that of a racing horse. Yes, I saw something worse, few boys with beards, a girl who had the worst earrings than those owned by my grandmother. I saw a boy who looked like he was killing himself with cancer sticks if not weed, and yes he showed. He was old and a girl with huge breasts than my ones. The first word I said was "thank god, now I can breathe"...so glad no one heard me.

The school was out and everything wasn't bad at all, my new classmates were not bad at all compared to what I've drawn in my head earlier on. Something positive came out of my mouth that day and that was by saying "I can't wait for tomorrow" yeah I said it I couldn't wait, truly speaking I wasn't looking up to anything that was bound to happen that day and that was caused by those annoying boys in the grade twelve classes, I had to do something about their behaviour but somehow they will bully me until I don't know when.

I'm A Misfit

The high school was already out when we got to the hostel, everyone was rushing to the dining hall to get food; that includes that boy who missed breakfast, I felt sorry for him. He was the first one in the queue with his 1litre lunch tin, the lunch tin was big, I hope he wasn't expecting the ladies to fill it up; what will others eat? I thought to myself. Thank God I've brought a plate or else I'd be wondering around and worried about getting food and borrowing a plate, the food aroma was mouth watering and I couldn't wait to eat, I was famished. The room was crowded and noisy, some singing, chatting and some whispering, I was just standing there and wondering if I looked invisible enough to finish, exit the place and lock myself in my room and dig into my food.

The menu

One small piece of boiled chicken,
Fried carrots that looked like Chakalaka but they didn't taste bad,
Then pap though it was stiff pap and had small balls like it wasn't stirred properly. I decided to follow Dibuseng my long lost cousin from Matatiele; only my grandmother can tell how

we related with her father, what was amazing is that we shared the same surname. My uncle had spoken to Dibuseng to look after me, he had taken her numbers since I didn't have a mobile phone to call my own. She did, however, promise to do as she was told after all she was family and we shared the same surname," I am old enough to take care of myself" those were the words I said to my uncle. Dibuseng was dark in complexion, average body, and had a stunning figure and mostly I loved her legs. She had nice relaxed hair though I found something funny about it. So Matatiele happens to be the hottest place in the east of the South African map, the sea is about an hour away from matatiele though we can't see it, sad that we can only get the sun. So basically everyone who stays in Matatiele can be easily be spotted, and that is by looking at the colour of their hair. The hair will look brown or I should say coffee brown, I am also from there and I've looked like that too, so if anyone can stay in Matatiele their hair colour would change naturally, without dying it or anything. Then in winter it also gets really cold and our hair doesn't grow and we would suffer from hairline disease or the hair will automatically fall off because of the cold.

Dibuseng looked like she knew the place very well and she knew almost half of the girls, I knew she was happy and i understood why, she was free from her parents which I happened to have known since I was young, she had to be happy, whatever she would do no one was to say anything that includes her younger sisters who come just after her, she was not there too and she had her own little world to look after and was totally given independence and freedom. Dibuseng was staying in room six; the room had four if not five beds. I think all the girls in there were from matatiele. There was Rethabile, Mampapadi, and Motshewa aka the Queen of Afro they called her. There was a girl who I also thought I knew; Dimakatso though she was staying in room 8. I was sitting on Dibuseng's bed whilst trying to finish my food, I seemed to enjoy myself and I somehow felt safe and free. Dibuseng started talking about my grandfather and how she feared the dogs we had, that reminded me that no one would just come to my home without knowing what they wanted, our Bulldogs were the size of an 8year old, and I once heard that they once attempted to kill some drunkard near our house- I was also sure that he didn't know what was he doing there too. My grandfather was very strict and straight-forward. That was Ntate Koali for you of course.

Dimakatso; Dibuseng's friend from home, she was dark skinned, a true African beauty, she had a dark birthmark on her face; she had a beautifully shaped body of an African woman and a small figure to go along with her body. I thought her face looked familiar, I then remembered that we used to go to school together back in Matatiele and we were both in a school choir by the alto row. Her voice was magical and always stood out; oh how I wished she would continue singing, she could go places with her voice. She was dating this handsome boy by the name of kgotsofalang, every girl's dream he was also in the choir, first time I saw a girl and a boy kissing was with maki and kgotsofalang, on our way to Bizana, a school choir trip.

Later that day few minutes before supper the girls and boys

were playing soccer outside, it looked fun but wasn't sure how it all started. if the boys got the ball from the girls they will have to play soccer if it's girls then netball would be played, it was interesting and somehow I found myself playing along and joining the girl's team. I had to put an end to the idea of isolating myself as I didn't know how long it was going to go on, I knew myself that I loved being around people and having a bunch of friends.

I caught the ball from Ditebogo and was looking for someone to pass it to before it slipped from my hands, I ducked until I handed it over to Nthabseng-one of the loudest girls I've ever met in my life, I don't know how she felt wearing such a short skirt and running around with a bunch of boys alongside her. "Hey you Mampe drop the ball I don't know who said you can play" Ditebogo protested. I didn't know if I had to reply or punch him right in his eye; thank god he wasn't close, I knew I was no beauty and the last thing I wanted was for someone to point it out to me, I had to blame myself for cutting my hair short I knew I looked horrendous with no hair, again I didn't have to blame anyone but myself, for putting a weave with permanent glue on my hair, I got sick of the weave, I had it for Christmas, it actually pissed me off to the core.

Tears began flowing down my chicks and all I wanted was to cry, cry so loud that the walls would start to crack- I missed home, I missed my mom and I didn't want to be there. God knew I was trying so hard to fit in but I was a total misfit, self-esteem was something I've lost from the minute I stepped into these schoolyards, I left it in a bus from matatiele.

Nthabiseng came after me and wiped my tears "don't pay attention to him, come play" she said. I hated Ditebogo from that same moment and didn't want anything to do with him; I couldn't believe that I even felt sorry for him that he had missed breakfast.

The girl in the suitcase

Just after the assembly; I was extremely excited, I couldn't help but pinch myself that I wasn't the only tall one at school. In fact, there were other kids who were taller than me. I couldn't count how many were they, I managed to count the heads which were taller and I counted up to twenty and some other heads too, I couldn't keep up as everyone was walking back to their classrooms. I don't know how many times I had to look up the sky and seek God's face. I wanted to thank him for not disappointing me and mostly I wanted to kiss him. I sent a lot of silent thank you's to the clouds above and hoped he was watching, I was smiling the whole time. I met all the teachers that day and I loved my new group mates, though I was clueless about everything and I seemed lost in everything that was happening in class. Thabang, a light skinned boy with short teeth, he looked very bright and I thought he was a math and science genius. We knew we had him for natural sciences and mathematics. Abel and Paseka were good in drawing sketches, well I didn't pay much attention to them, they were quite distanced, Thato, on the other hand, was, oh he was I don't know, he was perfect, perfect from every direction, he looked like a Greek God though he was a bit young no muscles were involved. I didn't know what Thato was good at, maybe his glorious looks, his mesmerising eyes, talking too much and laughing at almost everything the whole time.

Dimpho and Molelekeng were cute little things, they were so girly-girly and looked like a set of power puff girls though one member was missing, they were always together and doing things together, they were also fighting for their spots and Dimpho loved being independent and did her own things. I heard they have been friends since kindergarten. They looked like gossipers and I didn't like them at first, they questioned about my Sotho accent and thought it was hilarious. Knowing how to speak close to twelve languages was not a joke; I was fluent in almost all the languages in South Africa and have been trying the African languages and Hindi, though I knew I sucked in Xitsonga and Venda. There was a time where I was into Portuguese, I even told myself that I was willing to drop all South African Languages and speak only Portuguese. In my previous grade 8 class, I had friends from Maputo, Tusha and Lucia. I was so into them I even moved to their table, sometimes I could hear they were gossiping about me but I couldn't care less, I would mostly laugh at myself too, they used to do my hair for free and they did it well, they even told me that before they came to South Africa they did hair to make money back in Maputo. During break time, I decided to stay in class and fiddle with my pink pencil case, I wished I had a phone; actually, I was bored and was even scared to go to the shops. Some girl by the name of Masematla walked in, she was also tall though I don't recall counting her head, so I put her on number 21, she came to join me ,she had little extra teeth in her mouth, very slim, her voice was too deep to be hers, it was that of a boy who just reached puberty. She was kind and kept me company till Dimpho and Molelekeng came back to join us. Dimpho instructed Masematla not to ask me a lot of questions, I didn't mind answering all her questions, and she made my lunch shorter. The doors in the hostel were noisy, they needed oil, and they also became my alarm in the morning too. The girls didn't care how they banged them or open them, some girls would walk as if they just gave birth, they couldn't keep their feet up when walking to the toilet or to fetch water to bath. The past few days were not bad at all, I was getting used to the food and would manage to eat the chicken and finish it, ausi-Mathaplo told us about a girl who was to come to our room for viewing -she said she will be coming to stay with us. The hostel was crowded and more "noiser," all the rooms were crowded and people didn't have enough space to even use larger bowls to bath. Room nineteen was worse and it had its own different smell that wasn't welcoming, Slender was also part of the room nineteen that was how I established that some rooms had older people who might be in their late twenties if not early thirties.

Mantahli and I were getting dressed up and ready to go to the Dining hall for breakfast, there was a light tiny knock on the door and walked in a light skinned, short girl who informed us that she had come to view the room, she already had a blanket and a blue square bowl. She introduced herself as Kefilwe, we all introduced ourselves and she said she will be coming in on Sunday with the rest of her things. Kefilwe was short, I mean very short, with tiny little hands and the most breathtaking smile I've ever seen, Mantahli and I prayed and hoped our room was not to be crowded like the other rooms.

Mr Ks morning visits to the hostel became a norm, he always came prepared, usually he would leave his jacket in his office, his shirt sleeves folded and ready to put his hands to work, I didn't blame him, there was a girl by the name of Nneke, she was always late and was Mr K's target, he knew he would find her inside the hostel either dressed, behind the door hiding or still running around in her sleeping gown. Some girls would be running after Mr K and tipping him off, some would stand outside laughing at those he would catch from the inside. He made sure he hit them hard and warned them that he would be forced to come every day if they didn't wake up on time. I have to say it was really fun and exciting to see Mr K every morning, he brought so much joy and laughter that had pain at the same time. One of the days I managed to speak to Nneke, I had to ask her some few questions on how she would disappear into thin air, this other morning I saw her running to the toilet with nothing but panties on, a few seconds later Mr K came in the hostel, accompanied by Ausi Mathapelo, they went from one room to another, searching for the girls whom some were found sick in their rooms and some found behind their doors. "I normally hide under the bed or get into my suitcase, they will never find me there," she told me. My eyeballs popped out, I was in shock "what did you just say" I asked her again. "Yeah I do that all the time, just don't blow my cover ok" she jokingly instructed. I've never laughed like that in my life, I even thought I cracked one f my ribs. I do agree Nneke wasn't that big but the picture of her in a suitcase was even more hilarious, it was absurd. I have to say she really made my day that day, and I couldn't contain myself.

Thato, the Greek God

It was Friday afternoon, the school was out, Slender waited for me as usual, but from class to the small tiny gate I walked with Thato, Thato's house was inside of the stadium; I thought that was weird and began to wonder why in the hell would someone build their house in a stadium. Of course, I was curious and had to ask him, though at first, I thought maybe it was the same thing as of that of Ntate Matang-tang, maybe he was also looking after the stadium and cleaning it too, but that was impossible, he was still young and was at school full time. He then told me he stays with his grandmother, and there was just the two of them, and yes I was right she was the one looking after the stadium and taking payments if anyone wanted to use the fields. Along the way he asked me about Centurion, I didn't know anything about it, just that it's in the north of Gauteng province, I told him that I only went to Pretoria zoo and that ended there-i knew nothing about it. He asked me about Joburg and which school I went to and why didn't I know how to speak Sesotho properly, I was never taught Sesotho, I did Zulu and English at school and it was my first time to do everything in Sesotho, I mean maths was even done in Sesotho! I only spoke Sesotho at home and that ended there-i knew Sesotho very well but I couldn't write it in black and white, plus I thought my seSotho was perfectly polished compared to seSotho in Soweto or Orange farm, well that was before I went to Qwa-qwa, seSotho language is taken very serious. To my surprise I never knew that there were poems written in seSotho or Idioms in seSotho, they called them "maele le maelana".

That day Slender and I walked slowly back to the hostel, because in the morning we made sure we left our plates in the dining hall due to an incident that happened a few days ago- we missed lunch and dinner, the ladies had to leave early for some teachers meeting and the high school was out by 1pm. That was the worst day of my life, though the food was sometimes bad but I had to eat, my cousin Dibuseng gave me movite to eat for lunch and it did me justice. I spent the whole afternoon wondering what was going to happen to me and what was I going to eat, it was terrible. But later that day when I walked to my room I saw food on the table covered with Matahlis plate, six slices of bread and an egg wrapped in a plastic. Matahli told me that ausi-Mathapelo asked her to dish up for me too, I blamed myself always going to Dibusengs room before going to my room, ausi-Mathapelo was thoughtful, it was magical that she would remember all of us, we were too many to remember, but she did, all seventy of us!

We got to the hostel and everyone was loud and thrilled that it was Friday and no Mr K on Saturday and Sunday and no early morning breakfast of dry bread with jam with no butter. We changed and went straight to the dining hall to get our food; we hated our uniform as it made us feel isolated from the other kids. "*Ah Bana ba Mononthsa, Ntho-ntho otle koano ha o kgutla*" a short scar-faced boy said to Slender. Who the F is Ntho-ntho? Oh God I knew it was Slender's name and I just had to ask, she told me her full name was Nthofela also my grandmother's name. I walked alone to the girl's hostel and couldn't wait to eat my food; the aroma was mouth watering, though I knew I had to ignore it. The food was nice mostly because it came with a green apple and juice and it was a Sunday's meal.

Menu of the day

Fried chicken-mistaken for KFC and took my smile away,
Beetroot with no vinegar,
Brown soup boiled with big sliced tomatoes on top of the rice as the soup sank under the rice and of course small grain white rice,
Apple,
A cup of diluted orange juice (powder juice).

Nthabiseng the girl who rescued me from ditebogo, she already had a name, or should I say several names, they called her Skhwiff or please call me. the skhwif one was taken from a dance which was famous back in 2007, then Please call me is a name given to a 2cm long skirt, so in short they called her "please call" i also thought she sought attention more than a three-year-old toddler, she wore those short skirts early in the morning, hot or not. If she needed boys, that was not the way to lure them.

Chapter eight: where is everyone?

Saturday morning was busy, the girls woke up very early, doing laundry, shopping, cleaning their rooms and their corridors. I finally found out what a corridor was, it was another word for a passage, it sounded so foreign and alien like. Ausi Mathapelo instructed Mantahli and I to come get polish and soap for cleaning, we were instructed that it had to last for two weeks maximum. I had never in my miserable lonely life used polish on the floor or anywhere, to shine the floor, mostly tiles, I didn't even know where to start or how to start. I had to ask Mantahli to put it then I was to take it out afterward and shine the tiles, I then got a chance to copy what she was doing for the future and I didn't want her to know that I didn't know how to put polish on tiles. Later that afternoon just after 4 pm, the girls were bathing; the corridor smelled fresh and had different types of aroma, which were, of course, different kinds of perfumes. Meanwhile, Mantahli and I were sitting on our beds and admiring the job we did in our room, it looked clean and fresh, we were tired that we even found it hard to bath, but we had to. It was almost time for dining hall, we managed to bath and we felt much better than earlier on, and I swear we looked more like zombies. On our way to the main door, we realized that few girls were inside and didn't know where the rest of them were. Some of them were running back to their rooms, and some coming from the school gate while some behind the classes, I couldn't understand what was going on behind the classes, and I remained curious. One thing that surprised me, I didn't know that we had to leave whenever we pleased and go anywhere we wanted, what was important was that we had to come back on time before ausi Mathapelo locked the main door at 7 pm, it was heaven on earth, though angels were hard to trace. "Let us wait here" Mantahli instructed. I literally froze at that very same moment and did as she instructed, I knew why she said that, but I didn't expect it from her. Standing by the main door before lunch or supper helped a lot, we would save time, we always had to wait for the first person from the dining hall to warn us about the menu of the day, and sometimes we wouldn't ask but see what they had on their plates. That saved those who were choosing if to go get food or not, the funny part was that I didn't have a choice, I always had to eat, and I had to go all the time, even though I didn't like the food. There was a girl by the name of kgothatso, she knew how to keep time, and she was always first in line. Kgothatso was from room one, She was of course not bad looking, had a perfect figure, as if she was waist training, huge hips; though her legs were tiny, but hey she was a girl and she was a beauty. Kgothatso was our signal, she would come with food and we would see what she had and then decide to go to the dining hall or not.

Menu for the afternoon

Brown bread; no butter, no nothing
One boiled pinkish looking sour Vienna sometimes would be replaced with an egg,
Cold white tea,

We didn't have to choose...

Right after supper, everyone was gone again and the hostel was quiet, it was empty while sitting in my room I was able to hear drops of water leaking in the basins, Mantahli had homework and decided to get on it. I didn't have anything to do so I decided to go outside and get some fresh air, I left Mantahli alone. I didn't bother to even ask what happened to everyone and what kept on swallowing each one of them, one by one. The answer was right in front of my eyes; I didn't blink for about ten seconds. Nthabiseng the girl whom I admired so much, was sitting just far up by a metal looking seat; I think it had a water meter inside or some pipes. There was a boy right next to her; they were busy tickling each other, laughing like small kids playing with soap bubbles. I then got all the answers I've been asking myself, I knew where everyone was, almost everyone was dating someone and they all went behind the classes and the hostels. I became aware of that when I was from the shops to get sweets. The boy she was tickling was Mr. Scar face, Slender's cousin Monare; they were having such a good time and looked happy. Though I didn't think they made a cute couple, she was way too beautiful for him and this was no movie, he was never to change into a prince charming, like that of beauty and the beast. How I wished life was fair and easy, how I wished magic was for real. I was ready to change Monare into a handsome cute prince just for Mathabies sake, but they were not going to live happily ever after, not when ausi Mathapelo was alive. The weekend was short, I couldn't believe that i had to go back to school, I couldn't believe that another week of dealing with Abel's nose secretion was yet again ahead of me; I didn't understand why he had to always pull it back than just emptying his nose. Abel was one of my classmates; he'd always get a beating almost in every period. Math and LO were the worst classes for him to have ever experienced. He would even get a hiding from Ntate Mokoena, he would get it because of his smoking habits, just by looking at Abels' hands they'll tell you everything about him, it was either he smoked weed or cancer sticks. "Abel you owe me, my boy, come get your daily bread" Mr. Mokeona would say. Abel would negotiate to take his lashes daily rather than having them every day, I think Ntate-Mokoena gave him a lot, he would tell him to count.

Roommate number two

Kefilwe was accompanied by her brother; I think he said his name was Thabo, he then left after dropping her off. She was busy packing her clothes in one of the lockers we helped her to get, and her friends from class came to help her I think it was more of checking what she had in her bags than helping her. The girl who was helping, I think her name was Nthako she had perfect brown skin, and no ass at all, but I thanked God for her, she wasn't fat, the ass was going to show if she was fat, she was pretty and her skin was flawless, I loved her from the minute I saw her. They were busy talking about school and asking if they had any homework, a few minutes later a tall dark skinned girl came in asking if the girls did their geography homework, "You are lying we don't have geography homework" Nthako protested. Somehow she was panicking. "Mantoa is right, yes we do have and mine is already done" Kefilwe automatically replied. My first impression about Nthako was that she was forgetful and totally disorganised.

The breakfast menu never changed, I thought we would switch to porridge or cornflakes, but that was going to be absurd, there were too many of us. So for the next four years of my life, I was going to eat dry slices of bread with jam, baking margarine, peanut butter and we were eating them solo, if it was jam day it was jam day, not with butter or anything. And sometimes the butter would be so hard that it would stick just between our teeth. My grandmother always mixed the three together; jam, butter and peanut butter and they were delicious, she never loved eating tasteless food.

My day at school dragged and I couldn't wait for after school, I spent the whole day busy reading about the Nazis and World War One if not Two. The whole story about the starving Nazis drained me, looking at the pictures in my HSS book was traumatising. The guys were starved to death, some were thin and their bones were visible and they all looked alike, I read a paragraph that they even ate each other because they ran out of food. I could swear that they looked like Angelina Jolie and Nicole Richie, though their story is different and no one starved them.

My uncle gave me a time radio and said it was going to be useful, I took it out and plugged it in and it worked, it was playing music. I was busy polishing my school shoes-, in fact, I was almost done with everything when we heard a knock on our door, it was Ausi Mathapelo. She was letting us know that we will be having a meeting very soon about cleanliness and that she expects our rooms and beds to be clean or else she will be forced to take us from class to come clean. I then wondered if she was going to go to Mononthsa and ask for me to come clean my room, hmm Ntate-Mokoena wouldn't allow such nonsense, but then again he was a tidy freak so there was a 50/50 percent chance that he would let that happen. The rest of the afternoon we spent indoors, we were getting to know each other when I had to tell them how I was born and where. Mantahli and Kefilwe nearly broke their vocal cords by laughter, I had to tell them everything, I was born in a mental hospital in umzimkhulu in KZN, no my mom wasn't crazy but she needed help at the hospital as it had nurses and was close to where we stayed. Well, that's what I heard from my mom, they thought I was lying butI wasn't, I was glad they laughed at me. They then told me that I was also a bit abnormal, Kefilwe said maybe I've taken a soul of a dead mental patient there-well kind of offended me but I knew that I've taken a soul of an angel.

I was always counting minutes; our class had a clock hung on the wall, and it was right next to me, Mme Langi or whatever her name was, she always made me sleep. Her periods felt long and boring, I spent the whole period yawning and not keeping my eyes off the clock, somehow I even thought the clock stopped working, she would go on and on about sex and reproductions and how animals mate and reproduce. I only enjoyed math and HSS as it was taught by the funniest guys I've ever met, Ntate Mofokeng for maths-he'd always mocked Abel for everything he did. He would ask him to write corrections on the chalkboard and clean the duster outside, there was Ntate-Lehodi for HSS, he was a short funny guy, he wore glasses but never used them, and he would place the glasses right on top of his nose and look on top of the frame. He was a funny looking guy and had been from the day he walked into our class.

Ntate Lehodi made me laugh till my tummy hurts, and sometimes I'd swear it felt like I've been doing situps, he didn't want anyone to sleep in his class and made sure that it stayed that way. This other time he was imitating people who sniff Ntsu, he literally spoke like them and even said Abels grandmother speaks like that when she's high. Everything he said was true, but not about Abels grandmother, but I do remember my aunts; Ausi maki, Ausi Tabita, Mamtshu and Ausi Masentle, they will speak through their noses like were blocked and had sinuses that the doctor didn't know what to prescribe, though they speak seSotho when they are high. Sniff always made me sneeze all the time if they gave me, but to them, they would just stay calm and breathing through their mouths and wouldn't even sneeze not even once.

Streets Of Hillbrow

I spent the whole day answering people's questions, I told them that Johannesburg was not what they saw on TV, the glitter and sparkle were only limited and was there for those who are clever and rich, it was bad to live there. I might have had a good life back there, growing up in the suburbs of Melvin and going to the best schools it was all thanks to my grandmother's boss David. He took care of me and still do, I'd get Christmas presents from his wife Gen, clothes and loaded expensive pencil cases for school. Joburg was dirty, dangerous and smelly and I didn't want to encourage any of them to go there or to study there. Nigerians everywhere-selling drugs to small kids; prostitution was what Joburg was known for.

I remember walking in the streets of Hillbrow at the age of nine; I was with my Zimbabwean step dad "Gap". My mother was not at home and I had to follow him wherever he went, Gap loved me like his own and bought me everything I wanted. It was cold that afternoon when we passed by Diplomat or whatever the place was, there were two ladies standing outside the entrance. The ladies were literally naked and it looked like they were not feeling the cold at all, The other one was wearing a leopard print skirt too short I almost thought she was robbed her clothes. The other lady was wearing pantyhose; I was able to see the type of a panty she was wearing and its colour just underneath. On top they were wearing warm clothing, it was almost like their aim was to show off their thighs and buttocks. I was glad my stepdad told me who they were and what they did for a living though he didn't get into details, he just told me that they sell their bodies for money and that they got paid for showing their thighs.

Earlier that day I used Dibusengs bowl to bath, somehow Mantahli woke up on the wrong side of the bed and decided not to empty her bowl on time. that prevented me from bathing on time and so I had to miss breakfast, I've never in my life came across moody people and didn't understand how they survive without talking to people, I do have a cousin "Mpati" but i thought she was 90% better than Mantahli, Mpati would be moody but she would come back to her senses and be happy again. Mantahi would take the whole day not knowing what happened to her, i mean i couldn't survive for few seconds without saying something, i always had something to say. Normally what my cousin Mpati did was to tell everyone in the house shit, she would even do the same to my grandmother, if we were to be sent to the shops she wouldn't want to go and say it face to face that she doesn't want to. Every day just after school Teboho my aunt's son would get into a catfight with Mpati and it would end badly; they would fight and break some glasses in the house, fight on top of the bed and end up breaking it. Mpati used to bite Tebohos body badly; even today he still has the marks of her teeth all over his body and mostly his back and his ears.

How I became a stripper!

That evening I decided to take a bath before bedtime. I was in my short matching blue pjs, I was going to fetch water by the basin to make myself some juice. I ran into Nthabiseng, the 2 centre metre skirt owner, I heard she owned those only and didn't have anything long in her life. "Hey look we have the same pjs" she said. I smiled back and said, "yes we do, what a coincidence". I don't know how we ended up going in and out of different rooms showing people that we were twins. I actually followed Nthabiseng as she knew almost everyone and I didn't. I then went to my room and Nthabiseng was again behind me, she went straight to our window and started calling some guys through a window."mabekere good night, orobale hantle motho waka neh" she said, she was shouting and I prayed that Ausi Mathapelo wasn't listening., The guy left whatever that he was busy with and gave all his attention to Nathabiseng and mostly to everyone in the room, he was curious to see what was behind the curtain then he later asked Nthabiseng to open the window wider so to see who was inside, everyone in the room kept quiet as this happened and couldn't say anything or to resist for the curtain to be wide opened. The guy left everything that he was busy doing and paid more attention to me and everyone that was in the room, he had few books on top of a small desk with a 2 litre of water I don't know if it was cold or not.

He started flirting with Nthabiseng and asked her what she was wearing and he begged to see her underwear, "mmmm you look hot girl" he said. Nthabiseng just stood there and leaned her breast towards the window burglars and smiled like a lunatic. "Gee thanks boo; I look like this everything, "she said. if I remember very well I was busy mopping the floor as I spilled water when I was taking a bath, Justin Timberlake started playing in the background about what goes around comes back around. I found myself dancing and Nthabiseng screamed and said she loved the song, we then started to dance, we saw lights going off in Mabekes room which was then dark and we couldn't see him anywhere, we then heard his voice begging and pleading that we dance for him for which we did. He switched his lights back on and to my surprise, we had an audience, his room had more than six to eight people watching us dance, but we weren't aware, we thought they were coming and going out. Some girl by the name of Mantoa came running to our room to listen to the song as she heard it from next door. Mantoa was so beautiful, she was light in complexion, had beautiful chicks, hazel eyes and had an exquisite body, she was also from room 13 and there were two mantoa's in there. She asked why we opened our windows and we couldn't explain. Kefilwe was busy with her books so was Mantahli and they both were busy watching us. We ended up taking our tops off, I was wearing my black polka dotted bikini bra and Nthabiseng was wearing a normal brown bra. The song finished and we stopped and got dressed then Mantoa left our room as it was getting late.

Awoken by a horrendous dream I had about stripping and taking my panties off, it then hit me that last night I did strip and was dancing to a bunch of boys I didn't even know. "Oh my god what did I do, what did I do and why...oh God why" Mantahli was already from outside and said people are calling my name and wants to see me, my body froze at that moment, I was regretting everything I did and wished to die at once. My heart was beating fast and my body couldn't stop shaking, somehow I was feeling cold and hot at the same time. "Oh lord what have I done?" putting my hands over my face and wishing to turn back the hands of time so to do things right again. I knew it was already too late and I wasn't dreaming, I actually stripped for those silly boys and I had to face the consequences. A few minutes later, some girls came to my room to meet me. I've never seen them before and wondered where did they get the guts to come to my room and see me, why today it's almost a month being here, why today? "We just came to see the famous stripper," They said. Their giggles were the most aggravating sounds I've ever heard in my entire life, I loathed them that very moment and wished they could just die.

I had to eat, skipping breakfast was not part of my plan that day, I couldn't let a bunch of small boys to stand in my way, I didn't know how will I face everyone outside and i felt bad about the whole thing."God, please give me strength" I kept on praying more than hundred times. Fuck it I walked outside and everyone started cheering, it felt like I was an award winner coming down the stage holding the award for best singer or actress of the decade. I held my head up high; walked straight to the dining hall and Lord knows I tried so hard to ignore the cheering. "Stripper, Stripper, and stripper" the words were in my head in seconds. Ditebogo came to me and started dancing in front of me, taking his T-shirt off and stripping in front of me, Ditebogo was nothing but a bully.

The past few days I had a new name and I was famous, everyone knew me, knew me for my famous dance moves and my real name had been forgotten. It was flushed down the drain and there was nothing I could do about it. On my way to school the window boys used my new name 'stripper' and that is how I knew they were from the hostel, I was no longer Ngwana wako Mononthsaha but 'stripper' the famous stripper, I was never Palesa but the famous Stripper. I couldn't eat or drink even to laugh without hearing the name "stripper". I was only Palesa to my roommates and at school, I hated that name and it gave me sleepless nights- it was a nightmare. Dibuseng asked me what was I thinking and so did Malerato, an old looking lady who talked so fast most the times I couldn't hear her at all. That day she talked to me like a child and said I shouldn't be doing funny things. One evening we had a meeting in ousi Mathapelos room, I was scared she knew about the incident that happened in my room the other night, she went on about cleanliness and how she finds some rooms dirty and panties lying everywhere.she informed us that showers will be fixed, timekeeping was the main subject. The noise was one of them too, she actually had an A4 page with the list of all the things she wanted to say."Tumi, I don't know how will it sink to you that we have matrics here, and they need peace and quiet to study" she said. I knew who she was referring to, Tumi the noisy yellow bone. This wasn't, of course, the girls in matric agreed with their heads and some old looking chick from room nine agreed with a "yes". The meeting took long, everyone was complaining about almost everything, but noise was part of the list.

Thato and I became good friends and we would hang out together during the break and whatever free time we had, we became so close that people thought we were dating. We talked about a lot of things and he even told me how he lost his virginity, and I too told him that I was still a virgin and I didn't want to be one anymore. Thato would come to the hostel and we would do homework together, Thato loved coming to visit me and the gang was getting bigger, Thabang, Paseka and Thapelo would come join Thato to his visits to the hostel. I heard that Paseka had always wished to come visit in the hostel and didn't know how to, he had finally found the opportunity. Thato, on the other hand, loved girls and he knew that they loved him too. He esteemed being admired.

⬜

Valentines Day

Valentines Day was approaching and it was month end, all our parents sent us money to buy all the things we wanted. All the girls including me went to setsing. The complex was small and easy to shop around it but I was scared to death to go alone, so I went with Dibuseng and I bought a bowl to bath and made sure it was big, lots and lots of noodles, sanitary pads, two bottles of juice, weet-bix and some snacks with sweets. I still needed things for school which I got, including a blue skirt, yellow and white shirt, socks both blue and white.

Tuesday the 13th-february, 2007, I'll never forget that day. What a lonely day I had, it was more like a morning session for me than anything. Thanks to my new name I was still single, I was wondering how in the hell was I going to survive the following day, it was a misery. Everyone who had relationships was nowhere to be found, they all went to town to get valentines presents for their sweethearts. Now I got to see all those who were miserable like me with no one to call their own if I had to write a list it was going to be a very long one.

Everyone was standing outside to see who came with what and how big it was, the first one to walk through was Sebabatso, Buyiswa then Lesego. That entire group was from room three, they were tight friends, and they all had gifts for their boyfriends. I and the other girls were standing and watching one of the hostel's cutest couple Mmatli and Hatlile, they were busy tickling each other near the main door by the grass, *mmm what a strange way to say goodnight or I love*. I thought to myself. They were so cute and were carefree Mmatli was one of the boys who used

to   call   me   a   stripper   and   didn't back down one second. He was a tall dark young man who had a very impressive physique; he looked very cute mostly when he had to smile he had dimples for days. Hatlile and I were the same age though she was in grade 11 how shocking, she was short, with beautiful white teeth though I've always thought her body looked like that of a 13-year-old... yeah yeah though I knew she will look 20 at the age of forty which was what I've been hoping I would look like, that was until I saw her father this other Sunday, I then realised that the apple didn't fall too far from the tree.

It was Valentines Day and it was a Tuesday-how strange, I was in class, my body was in there too, my mind was not there, it was lost, all i was praying and hoping for was to go back to the hostel and look at the couples who will be exchanging gifts. It reminded me of the day i first met Tumelo my childhood boyfriend though we never exchanged any gifts, neither did we know if there was a Valentines Day. We used to go to church together, my grandmother and his mother were best of friends and that includes my mother and his elder sister, who later became my Aunt Virginia's best friend. I was going on and on about Tumelo and how i was not ready to cheat on him, Dibuseng and her roommates were fed up with that story. Tumelo was so cute and charming-I've always thought he was the South African version of Chris Brown, In fact, he was the only boy I've baby-kissed and dated till i was 17 and i wasn't ready to date anyone else, we made a promise we were going to marry each other.

My books were already packed in my bag, I was waiting for the noisy siren to go off, I didn't want to miss anything that was going to happen that afternoon. "Why are you in a hurry to go to the hostel? We left our plates didn't we?" Slender questioned me. "Dude its Valentines day hello" I automatically replied and she laughed at me. Finally, we made it to Hostel and nothing was happening, just the usual things, food-eat-lough, and play. Mantahli and I decided to go to the hostel and do something useful in our lives and that was doing school work, minutes after that Kefilwe followed us back to the room. Hours passed and we-we were deep into school working when we heard the girls screaming and cheering, boys whistling by the main door, Mantahli was so skinny that she jumped to the door without us seeing how she left her bed.

Together we joined in the screaming, the girls were screaming at Tefo and Olga as they've already exchanged their gifts and Olga was coming over to the main door. Olga was from room one and was staying with some old lady by the name of khethiwe, Olga was so beautiful and looked very kind and cute. Olga was dark skinned, had the most amazing smile of an angel, she was shy and very soft, I've always wanted to talk to her, she looked like she didn't make people sad nor did she deserve to be hurt, it then came to my mind that reason why I loved her that much was that she looked like my sister Sharon. She had her resemblance and looked half black and half Indian even though she was dark in complexion. Tefo was a chubby young man, chocolate and bold headed, his eyes were shaped in their own beautiful way and they suited him perfectly fine. Olga aka manana that's what they called her, she strolled styling to her room without making any eye contacts.

Hostel Couples

"I am sorry to everyone who will feel exposed... I did this out of love for all of you" some of us are married and I am sorry but we were kids and that's the fun part of it.

- *Tshepo mabekere and Malerato*
- *Nthati and Lindelani*
- *MMatli and Hatlile*
- *Nthako and Motopo*
- *Tefo and Olga*
- *Tumelo and Lesego*
- *Mpoka and Nneke*
- *Tumi and Nkweshe*
- *Thera and Tonda*
- *Itumeleng and Thapelo*
- *Sebabatso and Bongs*
- *Nkedi an lebenya*
- *Matlakala and Bereng*
- *Monare and Mathaby*
- *Tlaleng and Makamane*

- *Lerato and Mpendulo*
- *Tlholohelo and Toka*
- *Dibuseng and Maniki if not Ndeyi*
- *Mampho and Serame*
- *Diteboho and Lerato (later on)*
- *Tshokolo and Mantoa (friend zoned)*
- *Nthako and shogwa*
- *Nthabiseng aka Skhwefe aka 2cm skirts with some guy named nkosana (or was it a crush)*
- *Carly and Nkweshe (remains a mystery)*
- *Mashamplane and Malefu*
- *Rethabile and Ndeyi aka Mandeyi*
- *Tshidi and nkosana*
- *Mantoa squred and Nkwesh*
- *Vuyi and chaps*

Some I have forgotten but this is the list I was able to compile.

Popingwana

So everyone was scared of Nthati the girl in room nine as she was older and we thought she was evil, she also came in the hostel with gifts and no one cheered for her, we were scared she was to cut our throats with a hidden weapon I don't know from where. I first saw her in the last meeting we had with asui Mathapelo, she would say we making noise and that she was studying and wouldn't want to fail her matric. I loved her body and I finally had the guts I don't know from where and I said "you are beautiful" she smiled that day and said, "Thank you nana". And that was how I used to test how evil people could be, she was not evil as people would claim she was, but still, they despised her and used to say the devil can wear Prada. In class there was this beautiful girl named nthloboleng, she was the most beautiful thing I've ever set my eyes on. She had the figure for days, her eyes were that of a Chinese woman, they suited her, she had a star in her tooth which used to sparkle each time she smiled, her smile was amazing and we literally became friends and started calling each other 'my darly' Dimpho and Molelekeng used to laugh at the idea and thought it was funny. Truly speaking they never invited me to the shops on break times, Nthloboleng was the first one to ask me to go to the shops with her. Nthloboleng the beauty with no brains, she used to get lashes every day for not doing her homework or getting things wrong.

Back at the hostel on a fun Friday, I found the girls making jokes about some teacher, Mantahli said the lady was my aunt I don't know how they kept saying 'Popingwana', I didn't know if that was the name they gave her or not. Mantahli was telling me the story about the lady and what happened to her. Apparently, the lady teaches the grade tens seSotho, they told me she was one of those people who like the good life like the Kardashians and she mostly looked like a doll and vetoed ageing even though her wrinkles were visible. The story began while she was reading them a book named Motsuane; she was in front of the class and simmering the book to them. While she was busy reading her false teeth fell off and she had to pick them up and ran out of class as the pupils laughed at her, it was actually the joke of the year. I myself thought it was funny and I joined in and laughed. Then Mantahli said she came back minutes later, with her teeth back in her mouth and washed. She said everyone was now focused into her mouth and thought the teeth were to fall off again. She said the teacher asked "leshibeleng? lebona moroho pakeng tsa meno aka?" that made me choke with laughter, I thought it was just crazy and hilarious, I wanted to meet her the same time, I didn't want to waste any more time, I wanted to laugh at her so hard that I shit myself.

It was a Saturday and everyone was sitting outside under the tree shade and making jokes, they took out their duvets and sat or slept on top of them. Tumie was one of them, her blanket had Nkoeshe the boyfriend, Dlomo and her roommate talent with Makamane the boyfriend. Dlomo had to get a girlfriend, he was all over the place, they had so much fun and were the noisiest creatures ever. Dlomo was the worst he was one of the loudest boys I've ever met, his laugh was contagious and that of a chipmunk, he was crazy and was always fun to be around him. I myself was also outside and enjoying the weather, I decided to take a walk around the hostel and back, I heard a voice calling me, "Palesa Hey wait up" I looked back and there was the mysterious skinny looking boy whom I always wondered if he was normal or not, he came running to my direction as if I had dropped something on the floor and was rushing to give it to me. I remember shouting "Jesus.what do you want?" not only was I frightened but I was annoyed that the boy called me; I couldn't stand with him, not only him but any other boy in particular. "Who is Jesus? And what do you know about Jesus" that was just after he introduced himself as Walter, I did know that there was a Walter in Block B but never thought it was him, I found his question confusing, I didn't expect something like that from a black person, simply because we as black people grew up knowing that we have a God and Jesus, it was forbidden for a black person to be an atheist. He sounded more serious and his face said it all. "Jesus is the only son of God whom he gave to the world to die for our sins" that is what I told him. I didn't know anything about the bible but was sure enough that my answer was correct. I have to agree that I did go to church, but just for the fun of it, mostly wearing new clothes that I wasn't allowed to wear anywhere but church, town or even the clinic which I doubt that I was ever taken to the clinic unless I was seriously sick.

"Who is God? And if he is the father of Jesus, who is God's father?" Walter questioned. I didn't know how to answer him; he really did put me in the corner. "Look can we change the subject please, you really are making me uncomfortable" I pleaded. I was really uncomfortable and there was no way I was to sit and take the insults from him. I don't know or remember how I got into a conversation with Walter; never had I had one with him before. He was one of those boys who looked like geeks rather than normal, if I'm quite sure he had glasses and used to wear these huge rubber shoes at school, I swear the rubber under his shoe was definitely made out of a tractor tire.

"So Palesa, what do you think about a stripping pole," he asked me. I knew where he was heading; I wasn't expecting that from him, one minute I thought of punching his face, though I knew I was going to kill him. Walter was tiny; everything about him was small except his shoe size. I had to make sure that I turn my back and walk away. "You know it would be nice if we can hang it in the boy's dormitories, it would be nice to have private sessions too, think about it. I pretended that I didn't hear him, I closed my ears with my hands and sang a very loud song, I knew that was stupid and childish but I had to do it. I hated him even more and wished I didn't listen to him; I hated him more than ditebogo. He kept on talking till I reached the main door and closed it; he surely did piss me off.

Back in the room, Mnatahli was busy jumping on top of her bed like a small little girl, I was worried about her and shocked at the same time, where did she get the guts of jumping on top of the bed with no spring?. I did ask her that just after asking myself, she said she can still jump and it was nice. Kefilwe, on the other hand, was busy cutting her nail on top of her small desk, she loved being neat and I didn't blame her, she was a real girl unlike me. Kefilwe didn't want anyone sitting onto of her bed, not even her friend Nthako or Mantoa. Her things were always packed in order, her underwear's in one bag and that made things easier to find, unlike me, some day's I'd wonder around looking for a panty to wear and some days I'd go to school without wearing one at all. I did try my best to arrange my things but I had lots of clothes and the lockers were small.

The complex

On Saturdays, almost everyone would go to the complex excluding myself, but months passed by and I was no longer a misfit and I would join the girls. The complex had several shops and one liquor store, and again without forgetting the game shop, the liquor store was called "kwa-mavundla" he was the only one who sold alcohol in the whole of Mnonthsa village. The game shop had machine games, a snooker table and a Juke box which used R1 coins to play songs.

The complex was forbidden but we went anyway, we always had to make sure that we bath and I mean we bath like never before, we would dress up, put makeup on if you didn't have we borrow someone else's. Back in my days at the hostel all the girls were using the shoe brown polish as makeup, but not all of them, my skin was perfectly fine and I needed nothing on my skin; I didn't have a single pimple. I was wearing a white jean with a back opened red top that I loved so so much. I knew that mostly I was no one's favourite but knew I had a body of a model and was perfectly shaped. Tefo mananas boyfriend, he had a camera and was busy taking pictures outside. All the girls were off to the complex went to him to take photos before going. I also took a photo and was excited about it, I was going to give to my Grandmother, and we all finished taking photos and promised Tefo to pay. I was of course with the room six'es and eleven's, as my roommates went home almost every weekend, their homes were close and I understood that very well. I then took a picture with Mampho Serame's girlfriend, the picture was beautiful i hoped, but i knew it was. Mampho was beautiful and had a beautiful sense of style and sure made everything she wore stood out.

My hair was showing some progress, it was coming out and beginning to grow, I promised myself that I was never going to cut it again unless I wanted Ditebogo calling me Mampe forever. No one was going to do my hair and I didn't have money to pay any hairstylist, it was then that I discovered that I can plate myself using hairpiece. I'd done a great job in doing that and I looked like a real girl, some girls couldn't believe that I finished all my head but glad they saw that.

Matlaka from room 11, I loved that girl and she reminded me of the girl I used to dance with Thando, she was in Speedy's video and he would come get her from school for a video shoot, and she is now in a group called 'the Queens of dance'. Matlakala was short, had the most amazing body, she was fit and looked like she goes to gym everyday, she used to put hazel eye contacts, she was dark in complexion and I loved her teeth she had a little extra of them, her figure was so nice and small I used to watch her all the time when she was going to the dining hall or to school. One Friday night Matlakala asked me to do her hair and I said yes, I didn't want her to pay me as I was still a learner but she did. I did her hair in room eleven, her roommates Mampho, Itumeleng Notsi and Tonda; they were busy coming up with different conversations and laughing out loud. I thought they were supportive as they waited for me to finish plating Tlaki's hair, they were just the three of them and loved each other. We heard a knock that night and Matlakala said Mampho should open as she knew it Serame, my mouth was hanging and I was drooling - *how come that we were all locked in the hostel but Serame was outside.* I asked myself that question and so I asked Tlaki, I was told that all the boys' windows were larger than ours and they could slip out easily.

Tonda; she was tall, huge breasts, beautiful smile with a smooth face. She told me how she got there and where was she from and how old she was. She knew all my teachers at Monontsha and asked me to send her greetings, that caught my attention as I had to ask how did she know everyone while she was in sekgutlong. Tonda told me she also came to the school when she was in grade eight if not nine, she said she used to travel all alone to Monontsha and that she was the only one, she told me how lucky I was that I had slender to walk to school with. She inspired me and I knew that one day I was going to part of Sekgutlong and that I was going to pass and be a high school student.

I hated Mondays as I had to wear the yellow shirt that attracted the bees, the boys from the grade 12 windows never stopped and were joined by another class just at the end of the classes. it was now only one boy who would open a window and let me see him, he used to do that every day and yelled "Tally ngwanana amotelele" meaning the tall girl. The boy's name was 'paper' like a piece of paper, he would ask me to smile for him and I didn't have a choice as he would make me laugh. Paper had more gold teeth in his mouth than the Game; I wondered how it was possible that a student would afford all that.

A lady in room 5 Dibuseng, she was selling sweets and biscuits, she had a little book that had all the accounts of people who used to take cakes on credit. I would always go to that room and buy her biscuits, sometimes I would even stay longer than usual until I got to know them and I mean personally. Staying in that room helped me to escape Mantahlis moods, she used to be so moody and I'd say a pregnant woman was better than her. I then became friends with Tlholohelo and we would do crazy and odd things together, we were young and carefree, Dibuseng and Nkedi loved us as we would make them laugh all the time. Dibuseng dated a guy I don't remember his name, he was light skinned and had razor cuts all over his chicks, very first time I saw him and I knew was Zulu, I've seen a lot of guys in Joburg who had razor scars on their cheeks, mostly in Julies or Jeep, Dibuseng was so in love with the guy, they loved one another and they used to stand outside the school gates, of course that was the time before hostel closes.

Roommate number Three

One night there was loud noise as if people were fighting, and for real, there was a fight though we didn't see it. The girls who were fighting were summoned in ausi Mathapelo's room. She tried by all means, to bring peace in them as she saw they'll end up killing each other. The girls who were fighting were Dibuseng aka Doobsie and Khethiwe the old woman. I thought Dibuseng had guts to fight with such an old person, she really had a gut and it was definitely protected by a steel cage. Ausi Mathapelo then decided it was best that she separate the girls and put them in different rooms; it was still a mystery on how the fight started and why it started. Doobsie came to our room and asked if she could stay with us it wasn't minutes later that Ausi Mathapelo followed, we didn't have a choice to say no so we said yes she can come, she promised she was going to behave. Olga was the one helping Doobsie to move her stuff to our room, the room was now crowded and we had little space but I was happy that Dibuseng was going to stay with us as I thought she was crazy. Within the few weeks Doobsie had moved in, we became close and she told me she was from vosloorus, we used to talk about a lot of things and that included us exchanging things we didn't like or loved. She showed me her pictures and that of the rest of her family, her son Tankiso, her sister Dimpho and everyone, she hung Tankiso's pictures next to her bed so she could look at him all the time. I never used to sit on top of Manthli or Kefilwe's bed. I don't know why, but I sat on top of Doobsies' as I felt free, she was an amazing person and was full of sh*t sometimes.

Dibuseng dated a guy by the name of Kamohi if I'm not mistaken, she used to take me with her. Kamohi stayed in some of the houses far from Mononthsa, Dibuseng loved him a lot. She would take me to see Kamohi, she didn't care if I was there and looking at her man. She knew I wasn't going to take him and she knew I was scared of boys, I would say I seized great lessons from Doobsie about dating men. I learned that relationships were not based on kissing, sex or seriousness but friendships, Kamohi and Dobbsies relationship was sometimes strange, but I liked the guy as he would share his weed with Doobsie. They would smoke together and keep each other company, they would joke around, chase each other and laugh like kids , I even though the thing that brought them together was Weed rather than love but it was something very special, and I thought that no one could tell but themselves, I also kind of had a chance to taste weed and I only had one pull so I really can't comment a lot about it.

The rest of my family had put a lot of negative ideas in my head, mostly about teenage relationships and boys, I think they did that for my own benefit, and I can say they did a good job. I was the dumbest thing alive; I feared boys and wished they feared me too. Some gave me the looks and I tried avoiding them, sometimes I'd have dreams about kissing boys and I'd wake up and drink water or pray about, that didn't help, I was human and mostly a teenager and my hormones were raging. I happened to have been using a vanilla body deodorant that I bought at ShopRite, which I thought it smelled like heaven, it was a morning and we were getting ready for school. Doobsie went outside and said we are hurting her nose, Kefilwe and I exchanged looks and we frowned, we were no more allowed to use our body sprays."Ok, that's a first" she said and we made funny noises through our throats. Anyways we still used our sprays where else were we going to use them?

Olga started coming to our room to visit her friend, they used to go on and on about the room 1s and how they miss each other and how Tefo and herself are having problems in their relationship. Olga told us that she also wants to move out from there and go somewhere else, we then discovered that Khethiwe was bossy and wanted to control everything and that included controlling Olga's relationship with Tefo, I don't know how. "I hope they are treating you well here my friend, and I can see you having fun without me" Olga told Dibuseng. "Yes they are ok and I don't have any problems staying here" she replied. Those two girls talked about us as if we were not there in the same room with them.

The other night Mantahli was helping me with my accounting homework, we heard a knock on our window, we all exchanged looks and thought the knock was at the wrong room. Indeed it was in a wrong room, ever since we got to the hostel we had never had a boy knocking in our room. We always sticked by the school rules and made sure we were abidded them, "Hey wena, you're lost whoever you are" Mantahli said. The voice was asking for Doobsie and we had to call her to come over and open the window herself, she asked us who it was and we didn't have a clue at all.

The boy who was knocking happened to be Tefo Mananas boyfriend; he smelled of alcohol and was very loud. It was my first time hearing his voice, his Sotho was so deep and there were some words he didn't complete because of his accent. He spoke seSotho very well like a British guy speaking English, he was definitely from Lesotho and I thought that was just amazing, I was so into their conversating and I didn't want to miss anything they were talking about. Tefo asked why Dibuseng moved out and left Manana with that evil woman, he also asked who she staying with which she told him. "Oh o dula le stripper in here, let me see her" he pleaded. She then opened the curtain and he saw me standing and packing my clothes, I smiled and said "hi" to him it was my first day talking to him and that wasn't a proper talk anyways, all he said was "wow" Tefo's visists to my room became more frequent than normal, and so were Olgas visists they became scars. Something was going on with those two and I had to know what it was, I thought it was unfair to Manana that Tefo was now visiting Doobsie and not her. I loved Doobsie's laugh and Tefo made sure that he was making sure they came out, they'd laugh and talk about other stuff i didn't know about. One of the days I gave myself the guts to ask Doobsie about her and Tefo, she said they were just friends but i knew there was more to that.'

Doobsie had a friend by the name of Fedile who later

became my friend too, she became more than just a friend but a sister, she would always advise me what to do and what not to do. She told me that She was in Mononthsa before she came to Sekgutlong and she also knew all the teachers and they loved her. She used to debate and she actually made me fall in love with debate more than I had been, she gave me good pointers and said: "I want to see you in Sekgutlong's debating team next year" she believed in me, and somehow had seen that good things were ahead of me.

Fedile was a very kind looking girl, she was bright and always positive and she knew what she wanted. Fedile was beautiful and i think mostly her heart was even worse; she had a very beautiful body. she was staying alone and had told me that her parents had passed on, I think I somehow cried that day and she told me not to as she was ok. Her parents had left her with such a big house that had everything in it, she made sure that she kept it clean at all times, The house was surrounded by a lot of trees, both peach and apricot, she was all alone and couldn't finish all the fruits. I first met her when I was with Thato, we were walking from school then I had to ask Thato to talk to her for me, I was craving for the delicious peaches I was seeing on her trees, she was kind enough to even give me a plastic and get more for my roommates. The hostel didn't have even a single tree and it was dull and had only Dahlia flowers. We then started talking since then when she told me that she heard about me and that I've been doing some impressive stuff at school. I couldn't believe how news used to travel so fast.

Since the hostel didn't have any television we would go

to Fedile's house to watch Days of Our Lives while eating her peaches. Her house was our small escape to the hostel and it was also a therapy for me and my roommates, sometimes staying at the hostel and not going home depressed me and I needed to be away but I couldn't know how was I going to do that. Sometimes I would go to Fediles house to hang out with her or to run away from Mantahlis moods, Fedile would always tell me to come with my books when I come to see her, she would help me with homework or help me write poetry. I once told her that I was in love with poetry and wanted to try writing it. I heard from the scholars in Sekgutlong that Fedile would stand in front of the assembly and read a poem, she was brave and always stood out; I loved and admired her dearly, she became nothing but a sister and s mentor.

I woke up blind

One cold Saturday morning I woke up and I couldn't see, in fact, I couldn't open my eyes. I somehow had a clue of what was going, my face was swollen and my eyes too. I had to miss breakfast and hide; I knew what was going to happen to me if I had to go outside. The girls came back from the dining hall and Mnatahli asked me if I was on diet, I replied with my blankets over my head and said no! The girls were talking about going to the complex, I was interested and wished to go but I knew I couldn't go.

Hours later my face was even worse, I couldn't open my eyes and I had to pee, I asked Mantahli to take me to the toilet as couldn't see, immediately when I took my blankets off, my roommates were scared of me or to even look at my face, they were screaming, I knew I looked deformed like a Hill Billy freak. Dibuseng was the first person to laugh and asked what had happened to me, Kefilwe felt bad and said she doesn't have to laugh at me' though she laughed a little. Mantahli later joined and took my hand to help me stand, of course, I was able to walk but couldn't see the way, it was dark everywhere. I stood up and Mantahli ran away from me, I knew I reminded her of Wrong Turn the movie, she then went to the corridor and shouted: "tlong le tlo bona Palesa" she was so loud and I heard a lot of footsteps from the corridor heading to my room. My heart was broken and I didn't think it was necessary for them to actually call the girls to come see me. Mantahli then walked me to the toilet, I peed and I told her that I was finished, she took me to the basins to wash my hands. I knew that the looks will disappear; I knew that I was going to be ok. When I was younger I was allergic to ice and red meat, people used to laugh and said that was insane as the ice was water. My mother once took me to Hillbrow clinic and I got immunised and the allergy thing stopped, though she then wouldn't let me eat ice or red meat. Ever since then I've been avoiding that, but I couldn't avoid it at school. If the food was made in the dining hall and you didn't eat or like it; then you would have to leave it for those who eat it. Last night I was hungry and I couldn't stop myself from eating and i thought the food was nice than usual.

The menu that destroyed my life

White and well-cooked rice,
Braaid red meat with tasty Robertson spices,
Beef gravy,
Mashed butternut,
The usual dilluted juice,
Green apple which was a bonus.

The swelling took the whole day, I looked like I was mugged by a group of gangsters, my eyes were still swollen and that lasted for two weeks maximum. Both my eyes were bruised like I was beaten by a gang of drug addicts, the guys at school laughed at me, I lied to them that there was a pillow fight in my room and they stopped teasing me and thought that was just too cool.

The months dragged and some people moved out of the hostel, which included Olga, rumours went on about the brick she got as she broke up with Tefo and others said that she was told to stop dating him. My name as a stripper was no longer frequently used than before, I thought it was because some guys found me attractive and of course some of them tried to make moves on me but I wasn't into dating and I didn't know anything about kissing a boy. The girls would fight with each other, some moved out of their rooms and some leaving the hostel. Bricks would sit on people's doors and they would definitely turn people into enemies. oh and Nthako got a gold tooth, she said her mom got it for her, I remember that day she couldn't stop smiling and people claimed it was fake, I couldn't care less as I wasn't into gold teeth though it was a trend.

Tumi and Nkwesh broke up a few months back; she did get a beautifully wrapped brick from room 13 S. She didn't care, she just went outside, picked the brick up, read it and then said "thank you" in her loud chipmunk voice. Tlaleng her roommate was there to give her moral support, though she would laugh most of the time. They always had a stupid idea that they were going to get married to brothers and they were friends too. Makamane and Nkwesh were brothers and they were crazy brothers though I thought Makamane was more than just crazy, did almost everything together, they were also from Lesotho which was just amazing for me to see, such a wonderful experience. Some of my friends were from Mozambique and some were from Zimbabwe, so I was used to the idea of being around immigrants or so to say.

Ausi mathapelo would sometimes attend funerals and all sorts of things that older people do, and that left her with no choice but to leave us all alone and leave the key with the one she trusted. One weekend she left the key with Lerato the one from Room 13, she trusted her, she didn't know that Lerato was like any other girl who also talks to boys on the windows. Lerato would close the hostel late than the usual time it should be closed, all the couples would stand close to the hostel but Lerato used to give them time to do their lovey dovey things. I thought she was cool and she knew how it was to be a teenager and being in love.It was month end when ausi mathapelo was not at the hotel, the doors were not closed and no one was in the hostel but Hatlile and I and some couple of girls, but it didn't take me long until I was picked up by Maki and the room elevens, we went to the complex and everyone was so drunk. All the girls were drinking Smirnoff storm in large bottles,"don't you want to drink a little?" maki asked. I said no! And continued doing my business and that was looking after my poor drunk cousin Dibuseng. The music in the game shop was so loud and I had to get out and get some fresh air. Outside I saw the guy with thousands of gold teeth, he came to me and began chatting and he told me I have a nice body. He made me laugh the whole time, I really had fun that night but I was scared of the outcomes. There was an old man who looked more gay than straight; he would come to the complex just to dance and nothing less. Actually, we had three people who were mentally disturbed, abuti Sechaba aka Kgaitsedi ntlatse ka 50c,

Abuti Sechaba loved money and he was always running short of money, his throat was full of mucus and he would pull it and eat it up, it was the most disgusting thing ever. Some short guy with funny looking glasses who used to dance, you would swear he didn't have bones, then there was that guy who used to dance the same style for all the songs that played in the complex slow or fast he would adjust. There was the most feared guy by the hostel mates, his name was Oliver, I was told that he killed people and has been in prison more than a monkey eats bananas. I saw him that day and I thought he was just a tall bully monster, I heard that bullies look different from the outside but they are just little girls banging the door and wanting to get out! That was how I knew bullies-which they looked scary but they were not. I also had to be afraid of him; I did know that if he had to stop me from going anywhere but his house no one would come to my rescue.

I'm Gay

school was beginning to be enjoyable; my life was begging to change to the better. Thapelo some guy from a different class I think he was in nine B, I had a serious conversation with him and he told me that he was in love with me, I quickly took the idea out of his head and said I was a lesbian, it took me two weeks to confess that I was lying, he would always want to confirm if it's true or not. So I got tired of it and I told him I wasn't a lesbian but he wasn't my type and that I was into older guys with cars, money and I didn't do school boys, of course, I was lying, Thapelo was cute and handsome but I didn't have feelings for him, I let it sink in and thought that was the best idea to avoid boys.

He later became my friend and that was how he joined Thato's visits to the hostel, that was then he saw Itumeleng the one from room 11. He poured his out and couldn't stop looking at her, but he did that to a wrong person as there was nothing I could help with. I said I didn't know and it was true I didn't know what I was going to tell him, I had to tell Tumie and that was the only way. Tumi was more like me and she was afraid of boys, I could read it in her mind, she was one of the quiet virgins I came across, excluding me and Tumi the crazy one.

The months flew so fast that I'd swear I was watching telly track my horse, the season was changing and it was getting colder. I was glad it wasn't almost June and I had to go home for the holidays, the last holidays were shorter and I didn't spend enough time at home but at David's house- my grannies boss who is also taking care of my school tuitions. He wanted to know how school was and always wants to see my reports; I was a good performer, thanks to my moto. I wanted to be part of Sekgutlong so bad that I'd starve myself if i had to. He was pleased with the progress and said I can stay till matric, I didn't know but I wanted out of that place.

Old Stories

Monontsha's electricity would switch off and we didn't know why, mostly when it was too cold or windy, I was always afraid of the dark and couldn't sleep alone. I was thankful that Dibuseng and I combined our beds and made a king sized bed which was larger than a king sized bed; we would still cover our beds with different bedding but still combine our beds. That night was scary and we used candles to light, there was a lot of noise that came from the room eleven and I so wanted to go there which I later on did. The girls were drinking and when I got inside I was told not to tell or talk about that, I wasn't going to do such a thing and I didn't. The girls were hearing stories from the girls who were there long before us, they told us of how hostel used to be scary back in the days. They told us about a boy called boy-boy and how he used to scare them at night and break their windows, Maki told us about Phanga man and how he used to come to the hostel and scare them. I think they also told us about a guy who was found inside the girl's hostel and how the boys from block B beat him up all the way to the gate.

There was a story again about Maditopo, some girls say that when we were sleeping they could hear heels walking on the corridor and they wouldn't see anyone. There were those girls who would study only at night, trying to avoid Tumi's noise. Apparently years back Sekgutlong was a girl's only hostel if not girl's school, and the uniform was different. The girls used to wear green barrets, longs skirts, and the uniform included little brown shirts, not like now where everything is khaki brown. So the story about Maditopo was about a girl who died in locker years back, no one knew what really happened, they say the girls were playing hide and sick, so one of the girls hid herself in the locker and couldn't come out, she later died while trying to come out as she was trapped and suffocating. The girls said that the family didn't come to take the girls spirit; the reason why she was haunting the hostel and walking on the corridor at night. My first few months at the hostel was to learn and hear different kinds of words which I didn't know, Ditopo means heels in Qwa-qwa, back in Matatiele I learned that Ditopo means Gumboots and heels were being called dikwae-kwae

All my roommates were planning to go home including Doobsie; she said she was going to Mandela Park or whatever the place was. I was home alone or should I say room alone, I wasn't looking forward to that day as I never loved being alone knor sleeping alone. Later that night I was sleeping alone in the room until I heard funny noises outside my window, I didn't hesitate to check what was happening or who it was-Tefo knew that Doobsie left so I didn't understand why he was there but um sure it wasn't him, I was hasty about opening the window, which I later did when I saw a lot of boys walking outside, squeezing their bodies through the small buttlers, some standing outside. I nearly fainted out when I saw Tshepang and his afro-one of the boys my uncle said should look after me, to my surprise they didn't tell my uncle that they left the hostel and rented rooms somewhere in the village. He wasn't alone but with Toka his brother, they were freezing. Toka was the one that i knew not tshepang, during school holidays I'd go home to Matatiele and I'd see him, he was always being teased and bullied about his missing tooth, that includes Serame-Mamphos boyfriend. The girls told me that they both lost their teeth in the streets of Joburg, they had gold teeth and were robbed, and somehow the robbers saw that their gold teeth were real. They were both smacked in their mouths and the teeth came out and the thieves ran off with them

Tshepang and Toka told me they were hungry, they asked if I had anything to eat. I told them I didn't have anything besides coffee and movite, I made them coffee first and passed it through the windows, I only had one cup and used Doobsies cup, I didn't bother to ask them what they were doing running around in the cold weather, I then made them movite with warm mild and they ate, then they thanked me and left. According to them, no one knew back at home that they had left the hostel, and that they wasted the money for accommodation. The rest of the money they used to buy drinks and have fun with it, i heard they stayed at some funny looking place called "Animal Farm" i thought that was a book but it was a real place, the place had more animals than people just like the book. The owner made them pay rent, I heard he sometimes slaughtered some pigs and shared the meat with them, that's just a rumour still not sure the slaughtering and the sharing was real.

Witsies cave- My first hicking trip

6:30 in the morning the block Bees came shouting at our hostel main door saying everyone is going to Wetsies hoek, Lerato from room 13 made sure that we were all interested. I didn't even want to be told where and when, I took out my black Adidas sale pants, a pair of an old Lacoste tekkies that my uncle gave to me when I was on school holidays, one of my soccer T-shirt collection for swallows; it was red in colour with a VW logo in front. I was so excited that I was finally going there and that was going to be the best hiking of my life, all the girls were ready with their shots, caps, sneakers and water bottles. It was a very nice trip but I guess it was going to be a bit lonely too, all the couples were going, Carly and Nkweshe, Mampho and Serame and Mmatli and Hatlile; the list is endless.

We were hiking on a mountain top that had a small walking path, I've never been scared like that in my life and I was tired too. I wanted to go back but it was way far down and the mountain got creepier, we were all following each other in a row as the walking path was narrow. When we were about to the reach the top all the girls got so tired that we all wanted to give up, the boys motivated and pushed us not to give up, which we didn't and those with boyfriends were there to carry and hold their hands. Dlomo was also part of the group and was mostly there to destroy my precious life, he kept on saying "stripper climb that, you can do better". I didn't say anything along the way as I feared for my precious life. All I wanted to do was not to die there and put my grandmother in a misery, she had lost my mom and I had to be strong as she needed me to live. I didn't see where the path was leading to, but I wasn't worried about getting lost as Makamane and the other guys knew where we were heading to. He was there for Tlaleng his sweetheart 24/7 and made sure that she was safe. Tefo was there too, he was wearing the same T-shirt as mines, though his was white in colour, "so he's into swallows?" I felt sorry for him as Doobsie was not there, but he was with Mandu and was helping her climb most of the time. I was told that they were in the same class and they became good friends since then, they both loved singing and I just thought that was a good combination. Maki loved screaming and her voice would go ahead with it, sometimes I thought she would just scream unnecessarily.

Wetsies cave-it's a cave very cool inside and scary, it smelled of Patri core, on the walls of the cave we found a lot of writings and different kinds of names thousands of them, all different sizes and colours and different dates in which those people came to visit. The other one caught my eye that said "Thapelo Lenyora was here", I was eager to show it to Tumie and she smiled a little. It was a norm to write your name with the ashes provided in there, some names were written in paint, everyone followed the pattern and that was exciting. The cave is very far and I wondered how people made it caring paints, I think when going to the cave you shouldn't have anything in your hands it's a long way to go and very tiring. Wetsi is a name of a person, a Sotho warrier, back in the apartheid error Wetsi found the cave; he then hid himself from the white men as they were chasing him and wanting to kill him. The story was told by NtateTsebela; one of the most important people i had met in my life, he was also in the struggle fighting for South Africas Freedom, he also had a lot of pictures he had taken with our leaders including Nelson Mandela. He told us that Wetsie was a brave man and that he did things alone, he told us that he would steal some animals and slaughter them in his cave to survive. It was then that Wetsi was found dead and was killed in the same cave by the white men. That is how it became Wetsies cave. I got the honour of meeting Ntate Tsebala a few months back, i was given a research about the history of mononthsa, we decided to go there as a group, he was already an old man and was going to be tired from providing information to each one of us. I went with Thato, Thapelo and Paseka and some other boys from other classes. He was happy that we came to see him, he told us he was an old man and no one comes to visit him but tourists who also wanted the same information. He advised that his house was open and free to the public, he gave us a little tour around his house and we saw a lot of the things he had. He had taken pictures with Nelson Mandela, Thabo Mbeki and some tourists all over the world and a lot of newspapers written about him and his achievements. We were all finished writing our names on the walls well so did i and it was more than just one but four times in different spots, i was thrilled and so proud to have made it into the cave. A struggle song came from the top from some short guy by the name of Lekganyane, I've always thought he was a bit weird; he was my first proof that headmasters can be won by school kids and that they are expensive. He was then later joined by Mmata, the shortest guy who would look at me in the most weird way. He was short and had always looked at me in a weird way I didn't understand him one bit. All the boys were climbing to the top and joining into the song, they helped some girls who also wanted to join them. They then decided that we take a different direction and not the one we came from, we all climbed up to the top until we reached the top of the cave to a bright light. I had to say the cave was cold and dark but it wasn't bad at all, after all it was active and we needed the cooling after climbing the mountain, we had the most delicious water ever, it was flowing from somewhere in the mountains and it was clean and tasted very good with no chemicals at all, I gained some strength and energy due to the fact that we were now heading somewhere else and the delicious water did me justice.

We were walking on top of the mountains and nothing was visible but the blue roofing of our school, the place was so beautiful and there was nothing but grass and beautiful mountain faults, i mean all the different kinds of them and that was proof that the world was a flat surface. We went forward and everyone was curious what was before us, we came across a fence, the fence was separating Lesotho and Qwa-qwa. About few kilometres away we saw a shack and the most beautiful green pasture ever, the shack was big and built neatly, the boys told us that its a hotel for the tourists simply hikers. We headed to the left direction; I was leading us to the dark cave the boys had suggested we pass by before going back. "Everyone watch your steps and count yourselves after this" Makamane instructed. Some funny sounds came from deep down my throat like a moaning dog seeing a ghost for the very first time, the thought of walking in there gave me goosebumps. The fact that there was no other way, it brought fear in my eyes, I didn't know if I should shit myself or not. I thought it was the last time I was going to be around boys before I die, I've never been kissed in my life and i didn't deserve to die. Before dying I wished to have 5kids and be kissed more than once but countless times.

The place was was narrow, dark and it was cold, colder than the cave we came from, we could hear that there was water in there but couldn't see it. I heard Maki screaming and i knew shit was going to go down, Tlaleng told me not to be afraid, that gave me hope and i really had to see myself done with that. We all got inside following either, all the girls were in the middle, boy in front and some behind us, I felt safe somehow and I knew they wouldn't let anything happen to us. I was the seventh on the quaue followed by Tefo, I didn't know how many prayers was I saying at once. He held my hand till we saw a small light and we knew that was where we were heading to, I came to think about an expression that says "at the end of every tunnel there is light" that expression came to reality and I knew and understood what the writter meant by that. At first, I thought that I couldn't make it out, the darkness killed all the inspiration I had within me, I feared the unknown. We made it to the other side with God's grace, the mountains were beautiful, and we were literally on top of them. We saw a crashed helicopter and wondered if the people got help or died there, we didn't go close, then few metres away was a car that crashed on top of the mountains too, I wondered how it got there as there was not a simple road and no car can drive on top of the mountain. I told myself that I wasn't gonna come back to that place for the next 10 decades. We were walking back to the hostel, it was almost time for lunch I thought we were far away and we were going to be late. We had to hurry back down and we still had a long way down, everyone was in a hurry and couldn't miss lunch, we were famished!

"Ouch," I screamed. I twisted or broke my leg, the same leg that I always had problems with, I couldn't understand the pain I had and why did I have to break my leg, no one was going to help me, who will help a stripper, I thought to myself. I couldn't take it anymore and I didn't want to walk. Everyone looked behind with one glance and carried on leaving me on the floor. Tefo came back for me and helped me stand up, he put my arm around his neck and we walked together. "How can you break your leg this far stripper? You have timing hey" he joked. I was crying the whole time and it was sore, he helped me climb down till we reached the ground, and everyone was far way down and almost half way behind the hostel. "It's fine ill help her you guys can go on" he said. He carried me on his back and said I was heavy, I don't know how many ways he tried to carry me and failed, he would change his moves of carrying me more than a couple changing their sex positions. He told me to stop crying and that everything was going to be ok, he said I should be glad I wasn't dead. "Leave and go on you'll miss lunch I'll eat noodles or something for lunch," I told him. He said was crazy and said "who would eat that kind of shit for lunch after mountain climbing" he encouraged me that we were closer and that I should be stronger, I was pretty much sure he had lost some of his weight that day, he had to thank me later or I will.

I didn't know how kind Tefo was until that day, he was the first boy in block B I had considered to be an angel. I couldn't understand that there was a possibility of an angel in disguise, he carried and helped me to the hostel and asked the girls to give him my plate. He carried the food for me and delivered it safely to me, some boys were laughing at me and that included Dlomo, I saw deep down in Tefos eyes that he didn't like that at all, it actually broke his heart. After 1 pm the hostel was quiet and everyone was sleeping, i had to bath and nurse my leg. I later climbed in my bed and slept like a baby; I didn't have any painkillers to take and had to suck it up. I was worried about school and how was I going to go there, Tefo really helped out a lot and I felt indebted to him, if it wasn't for him I would have died or missed lunch and that was going to kill me. I spent the whole day asking myself questions with no one to answer them. Earlier that day I recalled asking God to take my life, but it wasn't a deal that he should put me in so much pain. "Dying peacefully would be nice you know" I said, looking at the ceiling as if I was seeing God's face for real.

The rest of the weekend I was nothing but a leaping frog, I couldn't do anything but I was also thankful that I was able to do my daily chores and that included my laundry and polishing my shoes, I was lazy to go to school the following day so I had to come up with a clever plan. I couldn't wait for the next day but at the same time I was excited, well well I knew that I was the best actress though I never made it to the Grammy's. It was a mission to get to school, my leg was sore and swollen, it took me close to an hour to walk to school, the boys in the class were quiet maybe they felt sorry for me or something. The first thing that I did was to go to the principal's office, ask her if I can go to the clinic or hospital. I didn't really feel ok and I started crying, I really missed home as I knew that if I was there my grandmother would have massaged my leg or do something nice to make me feel better. The principal said I should ask my class teacher if I can go to the hospital, truly speaking that day I didn't want to go to class, I was outside with Mr Lehodi-funny as always. He advised me to go to Manapo and see if my ankle was broken or not, my ankle was bad and I had to do something and not to take any risks. I took his advice and took the first cab that came past. So in Qwa-qwa there are no taxis but cars, the old private cars and there is a possibility of riding in a BMW 320. It was like using Uber before it was even invented, that was the only thing I loved and still love is that I would sit comfortable from and to town without any disturbance or hip squizzing. The cars were cheap and affordable, there were too many of them and they would come at any time.

So it was my first time going to Setsing alone, the only thing that mattered was the pain I felt, I was going to need some time alone to adjust to that. Manapo was the only hospital in qwaqwa and it was big, the taxi dropped me off at Excel garage which is now Salol, I had to walk all the way to the hospital, it took me 10 minutes to the reception, I couldn't walk properly. The service was fast and first thing was to open a file and was sent to a room that was divided with green hospital cotton sheets, a young and most handsome doctor came in and examined me, who later came with my e-rays and said my leg wasn't broken. I was a bit disappointed that I would be forced to go to school; the handsome young doctor gave me pills and bandages. "Look after yourself and stop climbing mountains will you" the young handsome doctor instructed. I smiled back at him and my feelings were crushed as he gave the look of I don't want to see you here again. Next time I really have to make sure that I break this leg.

The hostel was quiet and peaceful, I spent the whole day sleeping, I wasn't really sleeping as I was thinking about how I could say thank you to Tefo, so I decided to write him a letter and hoped that Doobsie wouldn't see it.

LETTER TO TEFO MOREMA

Dear Tefo

Hi, thank you for saving my life back there, I am sure that you don't even know my real name, but it doesn't matter, everyone calls me a stripper. Ever since I came here no one had been kind enough to help me with anything, which includes hugging me at night when I get my nightmares. You truly are very kind and I don't know how to repay you. If you need anything at all please let me know; I'd be happy to take the responsibility, that includes polishing your school shoes, ironing your school uniform or your clothes and i can talk to God about you that you should pass your matric.

Please don't tell Dibuseng that you helped me back there, and please don't tell her about this lettter...she will die a million deaths.

P.s my roommate likes you a lot
Thank you once again :)
Yours faithfully
Palesa "stripper" Lepheana

I don't know how many pages I've turned to get the letter right, but thank God the letter was not sent, what was he going to think of me, that i was in love with him?. That was the last thing i wanted to happen, and maybe I was going to get a new name that will last for two years or more, I was trying so hard to get rid of the stripper name and I didn't want to be called a home wrecker or husband snatcher. Everyone was so interested about the weekend mostly those who weren't there, some found love while others broke up, I realised that Tefo existed too. Some asked why Tefo had to help me, which was a mystery waiting to be unfolded. Some even encouraged me to rap a brick and put it on our door for Dibuseng. I didn't want to do that, I wasn't in love with Tefo at all, and Tefo and Dibuseng were not dating either. I didn't have feelings for him or anyone for that matter. The school was great, I didn't do anything, getting a beating nor doing something out of my power. My leg helped a lot, for the past few days Tefo have been checking on me and asking how I was, he was totally out of my league and one of the most loved guys at school. I didn't want to look at him in that way, I actually prevented myself from thinking over the fence. I mean even if I dated him, I knew that he was going to die out of boredom and loneliness as I didn't have time for boys and wasn't going to give him my attention at all. I heard that Tefo had left the hostel and had found a place where he stays alone, I thought it was cool; he would come to our window to talk to Doobsie as usual. His visits were sometimes scars, that was worrying me as I thought it was all my fault, thank God I never sent that letter, he wasn't going to come to our room for good, again I thought that maybe it was winter and he wasn't going to survive the window thing.

A lot of changes took place in our hostel as well; some girls have fought and had changed rooms. It was all a mix up reason why I didn't know if Mandu was a room 6 or room 8 first or not. Some were enemies and some became friends. I don't remember fighting with anyone but my roommate Doobsie, but it was something usually that even drove us to separate our beds. Nthako also moved from room 13 to room 9 with her friends, Malerato had moved as well. Khethiwe was left all alone in room one and Kgothatso had moved to room 19. It was a total mix up and everyone was everywhere, enemies were enemies and didn't talk to one another. The days of me being a stripper were also gone and everything was going my way which included my healing and was able to walk again. This other night I couldn't sleep, simply because there was a newspaper cycling around the dormitory, the front page was a bit freaky and everyone had fun with that except for me, the front page had a very freaky looking creature that looked like tree log that was affected by field fires, but when you looked closer to that tree log it looked like a creature, it was alive and scary. The headline of the story read "the lost Tikoloshi" I don't remember anything clearly, that creature was scary and I think I kept it in my mind to the point where i kept on seeing it in front of me. I knew from that night that I was going to have sleepless nights and I wasn't looking forward to it, and for the fact that Doobsie had separated our beds made my situation even worse.

The Tokoloshe

I've been struggling to sleep because of the Tokoloshe in my head, I did put a bible under my pillow, I saw it near my bed, I then opened the Bible stashed it under my pillow but still, I was freaked out. I then remember something back when I was still young; I think I was about six if not seven years older. I've always been scared of unusual things that happen in this life, I wasn't scared of the unknown but I have seen things before, things that no one ever believed that I had seen, not even my mother. Back in Matatiele before I moved to St Paul, that was when I was staying with my grandmother's sister Manchekoane , we stayed in a big village called kwa-sibi , it was divided into sections which had their own names. Back in the 90s, there was no electricity and I think that was the last village in matatiele that was waiting for the government to install electricity. Things that happened there were very strange and the people were acting strangely in a sense that you'd swear they were all instructed to stay there. Every afternoon just after 6 pm everyone were to be home with a closed gate, closed doors and sited, it didn't matter if it was summer or winter —we had to stick with the times. One night I had to ask my grandmother why everything had to be done that way then she said she will show me why that late afternoon she closed the gates, as usual, me and cousins Hope, Tee and abuti Zenzo stopped whatever we were busy doing. We had to rush into the house and not look back.

I've always been a curious kid and I never loved theories so I waited and ignored everyone who was to tell me to go inside, the whole area was dark, even the candles we used were not good enough and never showed any lights through the windows. About 100 meters away I saw a light; I've never in my life seen a light so bright like that ever before! The last time I've seen such bright light was back in Joburg when I used to visit my mother. The light came closer and closer, I wanted to see what it was, I was totally hooked by its beautiful brightness, I could hear my granny and cousins calling me to come in the house but I was so much into that light and wished it could come and brighten our bedroom. Minutes later I was pulled by my granny and she was busy shouting and complaining that I never listen to her in anyhow, I knew it was the truth but I was curious about the light. She then asked me to sit down so to tell us a story about the light.

That night we had a fire set in the middle of the house so to keep warm, back in the days black people didn't know anything about fireplaces, they didn't know that if you lit fire in the house there should be a whole somewhere in the house for the smoke to go out and not to harm our lungs. We would sit in there and cry because of the smoke and nothing had to be done about it though we got used to it. "it's been years now that no one knows what these lights do to people, but all we know that the lights that Palesa saw today was not human, no one lived to tell the story once the light come closer to them as the light hypnotizes and takes you away." My granny told us. I started by screaming and held her closer to me as I was scared to death. "The light that you saw lures you to it, you will see it coming closer but will not see when it has taken you, the light is hypnotizing and no one has a name for it. A lot of people call it the ghost we all call the light a ghost as no one knows what it is." That night I knew that I wasn't going to sleep and maybe for the next few weeks, at that moment I was even scared to go outside day or night I was freaked out. The story doesn't end there, when we first got electricity installed, it was around twelve midnight, my granny's bedroom window was facing the path that separated a huge valley and our house, that night the village was beautiful, there were lights everywhere, shining so bright like stars in the sky. "The count is burning, the country is burning" we head funny voices, voices that were worse than Tumies voice, they were to each other, surprised by the entire all outside. "You hear those are not humans" my granny whispered.

The brick for my roommate

Matlakala was going on and on about them going out to miss Uniqwa the pigeons, the idea was on everyone's mind, it was the first time the girls going out, they have been doing that quite some time, and the exit were the windows or the laundry room, if you were fat you better not come to the hostel, you'd have to make an obvious sleep out. Later that night everyone was getting ready and waited for Ausi mathapello to sleep. The girls were mafias, they didn't care about transport or what will happen, they knew how beautiful they were and they were going to get the transport cold or not. I kept on getting in from one room to another looking at the girls, they knew when it was time to be beautiful, and they made sure they looked the best. I was running around and hoping to go but my heart said no, I ended up in my cousin's room and sat on her bed as they were getting ready. Maki was busy dancing and she couldn't wait to party the night away.

I went to room eleven and found Matlakala was looking more beautiful than ever; Mampho was on the window trying to tell Serame that she wasn't going anywhere. Matlaka loved her eye contact-hazel eyes I should say, Tumi was just being herself, sitting there and doing nothing of course she wasn't going anywhere, she had a heart of a small chick which has popped out of an egg and afraid to take its first steps. Matlakala told me that there was a spy and everyone was talking it, She said everyone is aware of that and they will sort her out, I had to ask who it was, and why would she do such a thing. She then told me that the spy was me; she told me she was going to hate me if I did such a thing. To my surprise I just turned blue; I was furious and wanted to know who had such terrible suspicions about me. I was called a stripper a few months ago and now I am a spy? I asked myself why I have to own all these names. My cousin and my home mates were going with them, I would never do such a thing, I did however have the right to jump if I wanted to but I didn't. My night was ruined, my heart was bleeding and I didn't have any energy to do anything at all, I went out of my room and went straight to Dibuseng and told her to be careful, I wished her well as if she was going to die. The girls were all getting ready to jump the laundry fence, my roommate Doobsie was going to her own places I think. They all gathered in the laundry, some praying, some hugging and Makis face turned green like it was her first time going somewhere at night, she went to her room I think she forgot something. All I did was to stare, Dibuseng told me that the spy was Malerato and she's been warning the room 13s not to go anywhere. I later thought the reason why Tlaki said I was a spy was because I was going in and out of the rooms, I didn't believe she thought so low of me.

Mandu came back and said I had a phone call, I thought who would call as late as my granny was sleeping. I did ask her and she said she didn't know and I must just take the damn phone, I took it and went to the small dark room in the laundry, the room had few spare lockers both green and cream. It was dark and was smelly I think rats died in there, I got inside the lockers as there was no space. The last time I was in that room I was with my roommate Mantahli, the day she came where we had to look for a spare locker for her. "Hello" I said. I heard a deep voice, I thought it was Tumelo's, but I knew that Mandu didn't like Tumelo, but the voice wasn't that bad compared to my uncle-Di-wallets, it was a boy's voice. I then recognised the voice same time I knew who it was, it was Tefo, I didn't have time to guess he came to my room almost every day visiting my roommate Doobsie. He asked if I had time to speak and I said yes, my voice was hoarse, shaky and I was in shock. He asked me how I was and whether I was going with the girls or not, I told him no which was true. He asked me why and went straight to the point "I am scared what if I get caught?"

Tefo told me he loved me and he's been in love with me for a while, I didn't want to question him as to why he would say such a foreign thing in my ears, I was shocked and my whole body was in shock, I felt cold and I felt hot I didn't understand my body temperature anymore. He asked if he could come and see me, I told him my roommates were there including his friend Doobsie, she wasn't going to like the idea at all, but she was dating Maniki and again they were just friends. I told Tefo to call me back so I can ask Maki if I can occupy their room for the night, I knew she wouldn't mind Mandu and Tefo they were best buddies. I didn't hesitate and went straight to Doobsie before anyone else could, I told her that Tefo called me, all she said she said "go ahead he called you so why don't you talk to him?" my heart was pounding my rib cage wanting to come out, I'd sworn it was going to jump off my throat and straight to my mouth. "Where did I get such courage to confront Doobsies about that, i couldn't believe myself, and how the hell did I get such courage to speak to boys over the phone and even ask them to come to the window.

Mandu was in her room, all she did was to say what was I thinking, what was I thinking that a guy would save my life if he didn't care about me. She told me she knew a while ago and that Tefo didn't have the audacity to tell me, I thought "what the hell" why was he busy calling me a stripper if he liked me, strange way of pouring his heart out. I started having flashbacks, him coming to my room, him saying "hi" to everyone in my room, him asking Doobsie to open the curtain wider so to see who was inside, him not coming to our window anymore, him checking up on me when I had my ankle twisted. I told Mandu that I was scared to talk to Tefo, I told her about Tumelo and how I didn't want to cheat on him, she told me Tumelo hasn't called me ever in his miserable life, that ok I was the one calling him and he never did. It all came to my senses that Tumelo never called me but I called him, I was the first to say I miss you; he never did not even once. I thought Tumelo was the one, he never wanted to sleep with me, he understood that i was a virgin and he respected that, I've always thought our love had God and it was the love that God wanted. Mandu was so angry at me and said: "you don't even know what Tumelo does or is doing at this moment" which was true I didn't know anything about him at all. There was a light knock on the window, we started communicating with our heads on who should open and who shouldn't, all the girls didn't want to open the curtain as they knew who it was. "Just go to the window will you, and stop behaving like a child" Mandu yelled at me. They all went out one by one until I was left alone, I moonwalked to the window singing a mantra "I am seventeen and I am not a child and Tumelo never loved me".

I opened the curtain and there he was, the boy who saved my life, my Superman, my hero. I smiled at him and I couldn't contain myself, in fact, I've never been serious in my life, I felt like giggling if not laughing out loud. He said "hi" I opened the curtain wider, I wanted to see how serious he was, he was a little drunk and thought his scent was heaven sent only for me to admire. He said it again, the word that sent me to another season of pink and red flowers and blossoming green trees, he told me he loved me and he loved me from the night I stripped with my bra and shorts on. I couldn't help it but to laugh, I've never had someone to confess their love for me, the night was beautiful and he sure was the reason behind it. I never slept that night, all I did was to think of him,his smile and I loved his perfectly shaped teeth in hes mouth.I couldn't wait to see him the following day and I wished he never came at the same time too, he took me to a place I never knew I could reach. I glanced at my watch and it had been 10 hours since it was 2 am in the morning, I was all alone in Mandu's room, I couldn't care, all I cared about was that Tefo was in there, his scent was still in there and that kept me safe throughout the night.That night I slept with the lights off, door locked and no blankets, I told myself if something came to kill me I was ready, I felt ready to even die because all my dreams had come true; I had fallen in love.

Falling in love

I couldn't wait to tell my roommates about the weekend I had, the sad part was I didn't tell Tefo anything, I spent the whole time laughing and asking "why me?" a million times. I knew that I had feelings for him but I was scared and my uncle Tshepang was in my mind the whole time. Tefo brought feelings I never had before, alien feelings, not even Tumelo gave me, in fact he made me grow up at some point and I didn't care about anything at all. Telling my roommates about the story wasn't exciting at all, the thing is they were already updated about everything and Tefos dilemma. When I walked in my room from Thlohelos room, Doobsie said "Tefos Wife", I couldn't help it so I smiled, it was actually about time that I was called someone's wife. I mean everyone was someone wife and I was no one's wife. I followed her to the corridor and asked if she wasn't mad at me about the whole thing, I even told her that I wouldn't say yes to Tefo if she wanted me to. She did again authenticate that they were just friends and she liked Tefo, which brought a smile on my face as I turned my back and went back to my room. They say the truth sets one free, I am now confessing something too; I was seeing a guy, a guy I wasn't seeing at the same time. I didn't like him at all nor had feelings for him. Lehlohonolo aka Mmata as they called him, I didn't have time for him and I only spoke with him once and I never kissed him or shake his hand. I think I was mostly doing it to prove that I wasn't a lesbian or anything. I couldn't have his time; I didn't know how to tell him that I didn't like him and that he and I were not boyfriend and girlfriend. I've been teased enough and wasn't ready to be called Mmatas girlfriend, he was of course the same guy who gave me those funny looks back in the mountains before I broke my leg. In the morning to school I walked differently, my lips had lipgloss, my skirt was shorter, I bathed more than usual. I was glowing and I was in love, in love with a high school boy who I thought was totally out of my league and unapologetically hot. Slender said I was glowing and I couldn't wait for her to ask what was going on, which she later did and I told her I was in love with a "Lesotho prince" my knight in shining armour. That morning I didn't eat or drink anything, I was full of life and I was on top of the moon, he was tattooed in my heart like a prayer, hearing his name or voice made me worship. Everyone in class knew that I was dating someone by the name of "stevovo"; they had to know I had a boyfriend and the so called boy band I was part of had to come to an end. I was no longer Palesa the stripper but "stevovo". Nthloboleng my friend knew every detail and she thought I was in a movie, "things like these don't happen quite often my friend" she said. I knew what she was talking about, Tefo was naturally romantic, I knew he didn't plan everything he did, it was what he was deeply inside him, he was raised well.

Tefo and I weren't officially dating, I didn't say yes, I only said I'll see and asked him to give me time to think things through. I felt bad because I couldn't see him when I wanted to, I knew the suspense was killing him, he wanted a positive answer and he just couldn't wait. I then again wondered what all the rush was for, he wasn't going to die or graduate very soon. It was my turn and the other girls to sweep the class, just right after school as Dimpho reminded me, I hated the idea and thought it was just rubbish and a waste of time. I couldn't understand why the school didn't hire cleaners, Friday's were even worse, we would be given polish and just like at the hostel, we had to clean and put polish on the floor. All I wanted was to go, so I can see Tefo or something, I was literally going to die if I didn't see him that day, I wanted to tell him that I loved him and I wanted him to be my boyfriend.

The Strike

Just right after school, there was a rumor that Ditebogo and the other boys found worms in our food. That was right after I said to the girls the food was nice and we finished it all, I really did think the ladies had stretched their arms to make the food special. I ran to the toilet to vomit, I then realised that I wasn't alone but some other girls were trying to vomit too. Nothing came out and we had to give up as we enjoyed the food and had to suck it up, we went outside and were told that the boys have called for a meeting. Edwin the school president was staying at the hostel too, at first he wasn't. The boys thought it was a good advantage that he was also part of the hostel as he was to lead the meeting. Edwin was very hot to put it, his kaffir hair suited him very well, he always had something to say and was always important when he came to serious issues. I thought he was to make a good president one day, though he didn't have the looks of a politician but that of a Calvin Klein model.

Everyone was there at the meeting, everyone was angry including myself. We heard the whole story about the worms found in our food and, I even quoted that I saw that too and ate them live. We were out of control and honestly didn't think of the outcomes, the boys suggested we didn't get supper that day and said the ladies will eat it all to themselves. Just at the time for supper, no one went to the dining hall, at 5 pm the dining closes and Ausi Mathapelo came out and asked why we not getting food and no one answered. We then went to fetch food at our own time.

Menu

Deep fried viennas,

Brown Bread as always we never had white bread ever,

Tea that was always cold with less sugar,

Ditebogo, Mmata and Hloni were waiting for us to all get food, they waited outside the dining hall, on our way out they told us to wait for everyone to get their food, I knew they had a plan and it wasn't good at all. Anything that had those three was trouble, they had never been this serious in their lives ever, coming to think of it I remember Tefo telling me how glad he was that he had taken the decision of leaving the hostel, he told me about peace and quiet and mostly he could study, he told me how these troublesome boys used to be so noisy and destructive.

Everyone was done and we all had our food in our hands-waiting and standing as if we were going to be addressed by serious men with taxidos and paper work in their hands, oh well some of us were too loyal to use our hands so we had plates. "Girls and boys, this is getting too far and it has to stop" said Teboho. I didn't know what was he on about but I couldn't wait to listen and hear what he had to say, I despised him and couldn't stand the sight of him, He had made me cry in my first week in school and that was not part of my plan, he had made me weak and showed to everyone that I was soft and harmless,

I hated him so much. "You guys keep on eating this and saying they nice, have you ever asked yourselves why these ladies deep fry these viennas with oil? Where you come from did you deep fry Viennas? Do you guys know what is done to rotten food?" we all replied and said "NO". "Well girls and boys we are going to leave these viannas here because we don't want them and I mean everyone has to leave them here, you hear me"

Lord knows I wasn't ready to do that, mostly not while I was instructed by the naughtiest boy I despised so much, yeah I know people loved him and they were to do what he told them to do. Him and his crew started by dropping and smashing the poor pink fried Vienna's on the floor and on the ground and went straight to their hostel, everyone followed, one by one, there were too many Vienna's and thought of all the street kids in Joburg and thought they would have appreciated such meal in their lives than eating from the dustbins of Hillbrow just once in a lifetime, but I was too late and mostly too far from Joburg. Mantahli followed and I stood there and watched, she came and did the job for me "lahla ntho tseo wena" she instructed. We all went to the hostel, quiet and calm, it was like we were from the funeral, we all went to the dining hall in hope to get something and when we came back we came back with nothing.

I was back in my room son top of my bed, thinking about ausi Mathapelo and the other ladies, mostly thinking about mme Mamoloi, she didn't deserve all that and everyone knew that she was kind-hearted and caring, it was going to break her heart into pieces, I knew everything she did she did with passion and great intentions. "Banana meeting" I heard a loud voice from the corridor and I knew from then that the ladies saw the Viennas' on their way out and note ausi mathapelo, I knew how she looked when she was angry and I wasn't ready for that at all. She used to pout and look very serious at the same time. We all rushed to the main door as we couldn't wait to see what was going on outside, at some point I felt like hiding myself from everyone, I wasn't ready to be shouted at and mostly by Ausi Mathepelo, I knew she was going to look straight into my eyes when she's shouting at the other kids, she always did that and I hated it. "My kids, I didn't like what happened today, if you don't want something just come and tell us, we will also try to make things better for you guys and change the way we do things" she said. "She's starting with her English again oh my God" Ditebog's voice came from the back of the crowd, I knew exactly what he meant and to my surprise I couldn't stop myself from laughing and everyone joined in and mostly Doobsie joined in with her silly irritating giggle and she made things even worse. To my surprise everyone was there including my lace collar cousins Tshepang and Toka, I didn't know what they wanted from the meeting as they weren't part of it at all. Doobsie appeared from nowhere, the last time I checked she told me she was going to Kamohi to smoke some weed and she just appeared with her giggles, I have to her laugh was contagious. Ausi Mathapelo preached and preached on how our behavior stinks and how some of us here came to waste our parents money, to my surprise she even knew about David –I didn't know how was that possible, she said some of us were fortunate and some were lucky that we ended up being admitted in the school. "Palesa tell me how will that white person feel if you get expelled while he's busy paying your fees and thinking your studying but doing something different?" again she spoke in English, I laughed once more and replied "disappointed" ausi Mathapelo had her own way of speaking English, she would pull a foreign accent and remain serious, our laughs never intimidated her a bit. She was strong-hearted and I loved her for that... She was a hardcore, unbreakable!

Plan A

Plan A was not to go to school if you did then sewage on you in your school uniform, Slender and myself were included, the boys were angry and didn't want to reason with any of us about slender and myself going to school the following day. I have to say I was excited about the whole idea but didn't think that I should be part of it, I wasn't sent so far to strike, though I didn't like the food we ate somedays but I didn't have a choice I had to go to school. Lesego was telling us that she was going to go to school; she said she was writing the test and that she needed the marks for her final year end mark. I felt sorry for her, after all I always thought matric shouldn't be something anyone should joke about, and everyone's future is determined by their matric results. Early in the morning, the boys were already making noise, we all went out and found them sitting by their main door and of course with no uniform on, and some were still in their pyjamas. "everyone, girls come see what is happening outside" all the doors opened and the girls ran to the door, the first thing I saw was a twenty five litre bucket filled with sewage, it was stinking and Tshepo was right next to it, far down to Block B, The boys were singing struggle songs, one was a song that had Ntate Khumalo's name in it, I couldn't understand how they came up with the song so that fast, the name of the song was titled " I'm not the Khumalo snitch". They had made boards with messages written on them, one was written **"WE ARE NOT PIGS WE DEMAND FRESH FOOD"** the other one said **"NO HOT WATER NO**

SCHOOL". It was almost time for Mr K to come collect his own; I have to say that I couldn't wait to see what was he going to do if he saw us sitting down. We all couldn't wait for him to come.

Slender and I were already dressed and ready to go to school, everyone decided to let us go and said its better if we go and report the matter then we can come back if we did get permission. "Hey why are you all not ready for school? What is this nonsense?" Mr K questioned. As usual, he had his cane with him; I have to say he did look confused; it was his first time seeing everyone not ready to go to school. He was ready to whip everyone up and he surely wasn't tired either. "Don't you dare touch us Mr K, save yourself and go back to school" almost four to six voices spoke at once, he didn't even hesitate he just left us there with a smile on his face. The classes were about to begin, everyone was in a shock, mostly the teachers, and they saw that we meant business. No one came to address us, not even the deputy principal. Everyone carried on with their normal day to day chores, the cooks cooked, and the cleaners were cleaning and so did the teachers. We saw that the strike was going nowhere and we had to be noticed, we all stood up and started singing, we made sure that we made a lot of noise, and that was by singing the loudest songs and easiest ones so everyone could join in. we danced jumped and finally we were noticed. All the pupils left their classes, the teachers left the classrooms right after that. They couldn't teach we were too loud.

Our time for school was almost near and we had to

prepare ourselves, I have to say we were not happy about that. We were enjoying the singing and the dancing and mostly we enjoyed the publicity. Slender and I headed straight to the hostel and took our books for school. "We will come get you guy's a bit later ok" Mantahli promised. I knew she was going to do exactly that, Mantahli was my roommate and I knew her, she was crazy, manipulative and most of all she was very childish.We left the guys with their struggle songs and headed to the school gate. "We need to come up with a plan on how to come back" I told Slender. "I don't know what will we say, you need to go tell Mr Mokoena I am sure he will let us go" Slender instructed. It was a good plan, and I was going to give it a try, apart from us being from a different school, it was our right to strike, we had to. "Palesa please take your books and come with me" Mr Mokoena instructed me.He didn't get inside of the class but was just standing by the door. On my way out I heard some noise and I knew something was going on. Outside stood my roommate Mantahli, Kefilwe and the other guys from the hostel, I knew that the rest of the guys only came because they were curious about how Monontsha looked like."Palesa you guys are sitting in class while you know there is a strike?" Mr Mokeona asked us. I was shocked and didn't know what to say and how to answer him I just said: "we didn't now what to do". He said we must go with the other kids and make sure that we come back while everything is in order. Ok, that was fair enough! On our way to the hostel we heard noise and songs, the strike was still going on and we got there right on time for the first break, can I say that Slender and myself never had food during the break? Yeah, we never did. The guys once told us that they were eating bread that had palony, I was excited that I was going to finally eat palony, I didn't really remember the last time I had a Polony sandwich. The ladies didn't care if we were on strike or not, they cooked anyway, and the times never changed, all they did was to open the door to the dining hall so we could get in, and if it was time to close it they closed it. The school was out and nothing happened, the sun was hot and so were we .we sang and sang and some of us lost their voices, Lesego did finished with her class who, m she later came to join the struggle. No one came to address us still, I heard from the other guys that some of the teachers came to them and asked what was the strike for, some even said we did the right thing if the situation was the way it was. We were upset about that and something had to be done the following day, we had to have a strong plan and we needed it very fast. "guys, you all saw that no one gave us attention, me and the boys will have to think about this and come back to you guys, what we need to do now is to talk to Papa and Ausi Mathapelo, we have to have a meetings before just before we sleep, they need to open for us so we could meet up" Edwin the president told us.he was strong and he knew what had to be done had to be done. I liked him from that very moment, though I thought everything he said was too mature for his age. The meeting was over and we had to go get dinner. Ausi Mathapelo was laughing like a chipmunk; she was excited for nothing at all. "Ahhh shame, what a waste of energy" she said. I have to agree it was a waste of energy, we sang for nothing and the sun was hot.

☐

PLAN B

7pm:

"Girls…girls" I heard a loud voice on the corridor; I was in my room trying to relax and nurse my feet. I heard doors opening and everyone running towards the main door. "Girls there is a plan B, come…come" I ran to my door and Lerato Mofokeng was busy knocking and instructing everyone to go outside. The main door was opened as promised and it was warm and nice outside, the breeze from the mountains was fresh and calming.outside there stood the boys forming a circle and Edwin was in the middle, far down Ausi Mathapelo and Papa Moloi was busy discussing I don't know what, but whatever it was I was sure it was serious.

"Guys, we all saw what happened today, no one absolutely no one gave us attention, so we came up with a plan, it's plan B; basically whats is going to happen here is that we are going to wake up early in the morning and we are going to make sure that there will be no classes" Edwin and the guys instructed. So some other plans were discussed, things were getting more serious. Something huge was coming, I couldn't wait. In the morning around 5 am we had a little meeting, our plan was to go to the classes before Ntate Matang-tang opens the classes, we had to make sure that there will be no school that day, some of us went to the classes and put small sticks or matchsticks inside the padlocks, that was going to prevent Ntate Matang-tang from opening the classes. We then came back to the hostel and sat down, six thirty we all went to the dining hall for breakfast, as usual, no school uniform, dirty clothes and some didn't even wash their face and ditebogo was wearing his dirty and torn all stars as usual. Everyone had straight faces, they were angry. We waited for everyone to get to the school, mostly we wanted the principal more than anyone else, he had refused to address and we were quite sure we were going to have his full attention, the pupils started coming in, some in groups and somewhere transports dropped them off by the gates and some outside the gates. We started singing and more boards than the previous day; we were more in numbers than the previous day, louder than ever.

It was time for the classes to begin, I have to say the first teacher that went to the class didn't know what was waiting for him, all the kids were in the school yards and started everywhere, they couldn't get in the classes, that was of course before Ntate Matang-tang went straight to the offices, he was summoned by the principal to ask him why he didn't open the classes on time. Right after their little meeting Ntate Twala came outside to see what can be done; there was nothing to be done, nothing at all. The classes were locked and there was no plan unless they had to call someone who is qualified to burn the padlocks, and that wasn't ntate Matang-tang department. There was another plan, and that was to call some guy by the name of Lehlohonolo, he was from the newspaper 'Daily Sun' in Qwa-qwa, Edwin had his number and he did call him. Lehlohomolo promised to come over I think he was still busy with something but he did promise to come. I even thought maybe it was too early. The classes were managed to be opened but some didn't open, Ntate Twala promised to come talk to us- whom he later came accompanied by Ntate Khumalo.they didn't answer our questions. All they told us was that our boarding fees were too little and we shouldn't complain, the other guys asked if they are little we are supposed to sit down and eat worms or rotten food?. They told us that some of the food we eat we are being given by the government.Some of the guys who asked questions were mocked eg Mmata, he was told to sit down and shut up as his parents couldn't afford the money and they did him a favour by not sending him back home. "All of you here have problems, some of you haven't paid the fees and some of you still owe the school a lot of money, I didn't want to talk about your school performance it's a disgrace." Ntate Twala told us. " Lepheana I don't want to talk about you, you're in the primary, you were not supposed to be staying here according to the rules, your grandmother's boss, does he know that you are part of this too, does he even know that you are not studying but striking?" he questioned me. I was so embarrassed, I knew if he had to call Dave I was dead, he was going to stop all that he was doing for me. I later left the gathering with some other guys who were attacked by the same guy. Ntate Twala said he was to call all of our parents and let them that we were on a go slow. He even called Ausi Mathapelo to tell us how they cook and make their recipes, before everything else we all claimed to have seen worms in our food, but when ausi mathapelo was there no one said anything, it was quiet. We all looked at each other and pretended to have not brought up the worm issue. "I can't believe that all you here didn't come to us, why didn't you all ask what was in the soup? There were no worms in there we put a minestrone soup and it has small spaghetti or you can say noodles there weren't any worms there, is disappointed in you guys, you all know that we also eat that food" Ausi Mathapelo explained.

We were so embarrassed and didn't know if we should have apologised or not, I couldn't believe myself either, I couldn't believe that I believed the worm issue, who came with that shit anyway? i had to forse my fingers down my throat so to vomit the worms, worms that didn't even exist. I was disappointed in myself too.the meeting was then over and it was time for dining hall. I have to say the menu was good and it had mashed pumpkin with margarine in it, it was nice! We ate and licked our fingers. "This is the food we must eat every day" said the boys.

Walk to the Parliament

Nothing positive came out of the meeting, some of us even thought of giving up the whole idea and sit down. We assembled a little meeting and found out that we didn't get the answers we needed, instead, we were embarrassed in front of other kids, all our secrets came out, no one asked Nate Twala to talk about sensitive and confidential issues in front of everyone. "Guys we are going to the parliament, we are going to seek help from the parliament. We need to know what id happening to our parent's money, we need answers and we need them now" Edwin instructed. We all agreed to walk to the apartment, we knew it was far but we had to.

The parliament was far and it surely wasn't a walkable distance either; I knew that my leg wasn't healed properly and the hot doctor told me to take it easy and nurse it. the Parlament was about six to eleven kilometres away, it was too far, almost close to Town and it was on top of the mountain.we left the school singing, we were all wearing running shoes had water bottles, caps and some were in their shorts. That was the day we needed Nthabisengs two centimetres skirts, the sun was up and it was hot it felt like we were getting closer to hell. We were walking between the houses as we believed it was short cut, we needed toilets and we needed to refill our water bottles. The guys were in front and girls at the back we couldn't keep up with them. We had stopped singing, we were hungry and thirsty.

Some of us went in some of the house and asked for water, while some asked for toilets. Everyone was asking where we were heading, almost everyone we came across was curious.

We made it to the parliament, my feet were killing me, and my leg was aching. We all slept on the grass while we waited for the others, and soon we were all there at once. The security guard asked what we wanted, and whom we came to see, we didn't know who we wanted to see. He later came back and told us that we can't all get inside the parliament; we had to choose an amount of five representatives including our president Edwin. Some of us stayed back and rested under the trees.the wind was nice and cool.we waited and waited for a very long time.our representatives came back and said they were instructed that we must come back at a certain date and they will assist us. They said they were going to come back to us. I didn't really remember what had happened but a lot of things were said by the guys, we lost hope in everything. I couldn't believe that we wasted our energy for nothing. "It was a good exercise guy" Mnatoa said. I wanted to slap her in the face, what exercise, I didn't need any of that, and I was thin enough and didn't need any of that. I felt like crying and wished I didn't go. Our way back was very sad, it was something I had never seen in my life, so if you walked slowly then you'll be left behind, no one cared and I mean no one cared, we were all tired.some guys had money to get cabs while some didn't, I wished I had money, my leg was sore and swollen. I couldn't walk in my shoes but had to take them off. Along the way I was dreaming and wishing, wishing that I could see myself in bed sleeping, dreaming that I was in a bathtub with bubbles and relaxing. Tefo was not there to help me, he was not there to carry me, I knew that he would have if he saw me looking the way I did.i did shed some tears, but no one was to come to my aid, I was alone.

As soon as I got in the hostel I prayed, thanked God I made it. I went straight to the toilet and got hot water, put in my bowl and took my clothes off. I bathed and scrubbed myself and mostly my feet, they were dirty. I went straight in my pjs and got inside my blankets and dozed off. It was a long day, a very very terrible one. I wished I had a phone, I was gonna call home and tell my granny everything, I couldn't wait to tell her what was happening. A few months back I was nobody, I didn't believe that I would make friends either, didn't believe that I would participate in everything that was happening. Mantoa had become my friend, she loved me and I loved her too, there was something about her and I thanked God that she was kind to me. I had spoken to Nthatoa, someone I never thought I'd talk to her in my life, she was evil well she looked evil but she wasn't. I was able to visit all the rooms in the hostel and sit down and talk. Some of the girls were still young, younger than me and some were my age group. It was amazing, I was doing just fine.

PLAN C

Around six in the evening, just when I woke up, it was already dark as it was winter, we had plan C and we were summoned by the boys to make it happen, actions were already being taken, we all gathered at the gate, the boys closed the main gate to the rest of the school, we were burning tires and some were placed by the gate to close it completely. Mmata and Ditebogo came pushing a huge steel tank and closed the gate which was followed by a very smelly and huge bin full of garbage that includes our used sanitary pads, they stank like crazy. I was only there watching as I couldn't do anything at all,my foot was swollen and pained like nothing in this world, I was a leaping frog,the walk to the parliament was the course of it, I thought that was just stupid and childish, we went there for nothing as we didn't get any assistance and none of those people there took our matter seriously.

A few minutes later, Tefo was walking towards the school, caring his backpack, I think he was coming to study in one of the classes. he asked what we were doing and why did we have to close the gate, no one answered him but everyone was shouting and wanted to be heard, they told him to go back home as the school was closed. He went all the way to Ntate Matangtangs gate in order to get inside, somehow I found myself blushing for nothing and I thanked God that no one saw me, I was head over heels in love with Tefo and I didn't understand the feeling at all it was totally an alien feeling, I was sure it was something that my mom had never felt for my dad ever. Tefo called me and asked me when was I giving him his answer, I didn't know what to tell him, I wanted to hold and kiss him so hard and longer. I was scared of him, scared to just say ok or I love you more. That I knew that I loved him more and I wanted him more than he wanted himself. All I did was to

□

stare at his lips, I never kissed a boy but I knew how nice and tasty lips looked like and he owned them. Tefo was just perfect in every way, though he was growing hair and I kind of didn't like what I saw, he was hilarious and I thought of laughing but I couldn't as I loved him dearly and didn't want to break his heart into pieces.

"NO HOT WATER NO SCHOOL"

What we heard from our parents was shocking, the principle decided to add few spices to the news he told our parents. I was gain glad that Dave didn't know anything about it and was never called, again Ntate twala understood that if he called Dave then my life would be over, he knew that the opportunity I got was rare and doesn't happen to a lot of kids but I was lucky, of Couse I was lucky! How could I not be? everything was being taken care off, everything that involved my education. So Ntate Twala called each and every parent and told them about the behaviour of their kids and how they contributed towards the strike and breaking the school property. He informed each parent that their kids were in front and were swearing at him and holding big black boards in his face.

Firstly he called Nthabisengs Parents aka "please call me" he told them that Nthabisengs is a destruction to the other kids, her poor performance is affecting everyone she associate herself with , he then said they were wasting money to bring her to school because she didn't deserve it. Then I heard from Mantahli too, it was also confirmed that her parents were told the same things, infect all of the parents knew that their kids were leading the strike and were in front of everyone holding boards.

Palesa the lace caller

The strike had caused us our lives and we were not safe anymore, we were told to pack all of our things and see where we stay. I've never been so scared in my life; I didn't know where to go or whom to stay with. I didn't have money to buy food knor did I have money to pay rent to wherever I was going to stay. Some were lucky as they found a place to stay and some went home and some took their friends along. None of my roommates offered to help me, they knew Joburg was far and I didn't have anyone to go to. Doobsie was to go to her boyfriend Motebang, She had made plans already and that was leaving before the hostel became empty. I didn't know what to do or where to go, i was even afraid to call home, i knew if i told Devid he was going to murder me and cut me off, my granny was going to get a heart attack, my uncle was going to catch the next taxi to come to kill me, finally his dream was to come true, I couldn't call Gen either she was never going to stop buying me clothes or the pretty things I normally got.

Dibuseng had asked maniki her current boyfriend if he can help her with a place to stay, his grandmother was staying alone and had an extra room with a bed she wasn't using. He asked her if a couple of nice girls can come use it for time being. Dibuseng, Carly,Malefu, Mandu and Tlaleng who her parents later came to fetch her were given the room at manikis grandmother.I of course was offered to follow which i did and we all stayed together, all my worries came to an end and was back to my senses.

Everyone had left the hostel and some were staying with their boyfriends, some went to the animal farm, and some went to where Tefo was staying. I think a lot of boys went to Tefo's place, Makamane, nkwesh, Dlomo, Lehohonolo, Mmatli, Ditebogo and Lekhanyane, although they didn't stay there all together, There were some boys from Bethlehem who were staying there and they shared the boys. I was worried that Tefo's food was to be finished before time, I was sure that he wasn't buying food enough for more than one person.

We never cooked, we didn't have a stove or pots to cook, we used to eat fat cakes, cheap bread, palony and achar every day and I was tired of it. The water was cold and we had to keep warm, we would combine all our blankets and sleep together, I was amongst the girls who stole the hostel mattres, I felt like I had to, after all, David paid for it and I had the right to take it. I slept peacefully on the floor and was enjoying my stay. We settled quite well and we didn't have any problems besides my financial issue of not being sent money on time.

One night my roommates decided to pay Tefo a visit, it wasn't a visit as such but we heard Tefo had a TV and we missed watching Generations, Mandu said it will again benefit me as I will see Tefo. I was scared to even walk through the gates, after what I did to him he was going to kill me. I didn't tell Tefo about Mmata, he deserved to know and I kept it from him, somehow I knew that he knew. The Block Bees and Block A's had a beef but not everyone had, but the girls used to call the boys "Basadi" they behaved like women and they used to gossip a lot, there was nothing that they didn't know about us and they knew almost everything like who dated whom and who was and was not a virgin. So I knew that Tefo knew about mmata. We found Tefo cooking, the other guys were sitting down as the news were finishing. The room smelled nice of the aroma of well-cooked pap and Bore worse, my stomach was growling and i thanked God no one heard it, come to think of food I hadn't had a home-cooked meal for days now and I didn't feel or look healthy at all. Tefo was forever smiling and looking at me the whole time if only he knew how hungry I was he wouldn't have smiled like a mad person. We were watching Generations when Lumka was busy kissing Vuyo, the boys screamed and Dlomo said "girls lets play that thing" I knew he was just being silly but we all smiled and said no! I wondered who he wanted to kiss as there was no one who would agree to kiss such a silly and irritating human being as he was.

All I wanted that night was to be with Tefo, in fact the whole night, holding him tight and making sure he doesn't slip in my hold. I wanted to be with him so so bad, wanted him to kiss me and tell me everything was going to be ok. I loved his words and loved his voice even more mostly when he said "I love you Mbali" those words made me to belong and feel alive. Mandu and Dlomo kept on teasing us and said I must go sit next to Tefo and said she was going to leave me behind as there was enough space for my sleep. As much as I feared my uncle Tshepang, I was ready to disobey him. That night I was ready to do anything for Tefo, I was ready to let him hold me, ready to

lose the most precious thing in my life to him "my virginity"
Carley and Nkweshe were looking cozy next to each other,
while I felt sorry for Makamane, I hated what Tlalengs parents
did by taking her away from him, Tlaleng was excited that she
was going to spend enough time with her sweetheart without
hearing "banana ausi Mathapelo oya kwala" I was sure that
Makamane was heartbroken as I was, his sweetheart was gone
but it made me smile a little as he was going to see him at
school. Movhango was finished and we had to go back and
sleep, tomorrow was again another day for school and the girls
would have to wake up very early to walk to school. The boys
walked us back to our new home, I was front on the line.i was
trying to avoid Tefo who was of course talking to Mandu and i
was certain they were talking about me the whole time, we were
close to the gate when Mandu said Tefo wanted to talk to me.
There he was looking into my eyes as if looking for something
while I was there with him, Tefo was in front of me, his scent
was near me and I could smell him-it warmed my heart, I was
shaking the whole time and scared I didn't know why. My heart
wanted to hold and kiss him long and hard, but my body was
stiff like that of a newly installed electrical pole.

   "Are you cold? Let me hold you" he said. Opening his
arms for me, I slipped in and he held me so tight and I felt safe
at once. It was the most amazing experience, I loved him and he
loved me too. He wanted me safe and that was how I felt in his
arms. He then kissed my forehead and said those famous words
of his "I love you, please know that" tefo cared about me a lot
and I was thankful for that. He was my prince charming, I was

his Juliet he was my Romeo. He was everything I've ever dreamt of, the romance that i had dreamt of was finally for me. I didn't want the night to end, I felt like time was flying, I wanted to hold the life of my life till morning and I couldn't.

Not far from us stood Nkwesh and Carly, I've always thought they looked cute together. I was glad Nkwesh was there and was waiting mostly for us to finish, I didn't want Tefo to travel all alone, I didn't want anything to happen to him.it would kill me if i had to go back with him and protect him from a fly or even a cockroach i was going to do so. I loved him so so much and he knew that he was my first love, my first kiss and he became my world that night in Mandus room. I know the bibles states that it is a sin to love another more than God, which made me feel bad but I couldn't help it and I had to pray about that.

The school was not normal, everyone was on the hostel case and asking how was I coping. Truly speaking I didn't care what was I going through, all I cared about was that Tefo was there for me and he loved me back. I wasn't concentrating very well in class, I was always caught day dreaming. That day Ntate Mokoena asked if I needed help and if I was ok, I was feeling ok though I knew I wasn't eating well and wasn't having proper meals. "You don't look ok Palesa and you look like a hobbo" Dimpho told me, as much as I hated her I loved her for always telling the truth. No matter how much I tried to bath, wash my hair, wash my socks or polish my shoes, there was something about me that didn't look normal at all, I was dirty and I felt dirty too but I couldn't care less.

the thought of my grandmother not sending me money was unacceptable, I knew she was struggling to make ends meet, but i felt neglected that they didn't even bother to send me even R200, my uncles were getting paid every fortnight but they never bothered. I've gotten used to not getting money on time and I wasn't bothered, but this time I had to, as much as Mandu and Dibuseng knew me, it wasn't their responsibility to make sure that I had to eat. They used to buy food the whole time, sometimes I saw it in their eyes that they wondered when was I going to contribute.

Watching tv at Tefo's became an everyday thing, being with him everyday warmed my heart, he always made sure that the love he had for me was visible through his eyes for me to see, i thought Tefo was a hopeless romantic just like me. Every day after school I'd travel with some girls who stay near me, Fikile, Nomasela and Lebohang and some other girls I don't remember their names. We always had fun on our way back from school, talked about boyfriends and mostly Tefo was part of everything.

Ntate twala had given everyone letters to give to our parents; i wondered who in my family would travel all the way from Johannesburg to that meeting. I didn't have a clue that was going to be there for me and sign the form, i didn't have a choice but to tell my principal mme-Motaung, she was a woman of integrity and she would know what to do. She said she was going to go there and she would sign the form on my parent's behalf. I thought it was kind of her to waste her time for me and I'd be forever thankful to her, I was glad that I told her that

I needed someone. Right after school the meeting had started and we had to rush to Sekgutlong, all the parents were there but we were not allowed to get inside, Nnate Twala was scared of us, he knew what we were capable off. The last meeting he held during strike was a bad experience for him; we formed a circle and put him and Ntate Khumalo in the middle. We had boards written we needed hot water, good food and mostly clean and newly renovated hostels. Everyone was waiting impatiently outside, waiting for the meeting to finish, the suspense killed us, and we chewed our nails till there was nothing left to chew. Since Edwin was part of the student council, we were lucky he was in there too and was part of us.

The meeting was finished, the parents were disappointed in us, some came out shaking their heads and some were unhappy while others thought we did the right thing. We all rushed to them for information, the news we heard were not good at all. Ntate Thwala had decided that we don't have to stay at the hostel on weekends; he told the parents that the food we ate was expensive and said we did unspeakable things on weekends. I ran to Mme Motaung to thank her for coming, she also filled me up with some information. She said she wanted my grandmother's phone numbers, and needed to discuss something with her. Some parents were upset about the decision that was taken, they lived far from qwaqwa and said they couldn't afford for their kids to come home every weekend. Some were excited about the whole thing; they knew what we did on weekends. Rules were stipulated and there was nothing we could have done to change Ntate-Twal's decision, I knew

Dave would not accept the idea and grandma would bring me back and study in Joburg. How was I going to survive without Tefo? He was my life now; I wanted to be where he was.

Going Back to the Hostel

We were told to go back to the hostel, I was the first one to go back, I missed the horrible food, and I certainly missed eating pap and milk. The milk that the boys witnessed being dilluted with water, that was such a drama. I took all that I had back and made my bed and packed all my clothes back in my locker. Everyone came back that late afternoon and some were still missing, we were really happy to go back. After the entire hostel was our home and we felt safe in it. Everyone came back, but only to bring their clothes and went back to where they were, after all, it was weekend and they needed the freedom. There was a famous DJ that was coming to Stanville, everyone was excited about the freedom they had and they knew no one was to question them. It was their last weekend being free, and they deserved the weekend. The matrics were about to start their exams and they had to study.

That Saturday everyone was preparing for the big night, everyone was at the complex including myself and Tefo. Toka and Tshepang had bought me a cold drink; I think they were also sent some money. The Hostel boys were sitting next to the Pakistan shop and drinking so was Tefo, I have to tell the truth I loved my boyfriend when he was drunk, he always told me the truth. It was almost time for supper, everyone was moving, and we knew we were going to come back. Tefo walked me to the hostel he was hungry and told me we were going to eat together, whether I liked it or not. All the way to the hostel I was laughing like a lunatic, Tefo was wearing his favourite swallows t-shirt and his black Guess jeans and white all star half boot, he looked really hot and I was glad he was my boyfriend and I loved his sense of style. My baby was drunk, he went on and on of how tall I was and that me and him would make a crazy and funny married couple, "but I love you though, just the way you are Mbali tall or not I love you" he told me. I knew he meant every word he said and I loved him for that. "Telele" he called me. His arm was around my neck and mines around his waist, I have to agree that I was taller than him but he was chubby and I wasn't. "Hake Telele, and oh that is a very offensive name to call me by the way" I complained, we both laughed as we continued to walk to the hostel. Other scholars were behind us and some couples too. I was scared of me and thanked God for bringing true love to me at the wrong time but I prayed and told him he had to keep us that way till we both finish school.

I took my green flowered plate and went straight to the dining hall, Tefo waited for me to come back "hurry up, um hungry" he shouted. Mampabadi was the fifth on the row and there walked in Ditebogo and he stood in front of everyone. Mapabadi was pissed, she told Ditebogo to stand behind everyone as he was late. "Stop talking too much, you are too short for this nonsense" he said. He then said Mampabadi had a huge head and if she had to look at the sky her head will pull her down and she would fall, everyone laughed so hard, I didn't want to laugh at him, I didn't have a choice but to laugh at him, he was stupid and spoke like a child.

☐

<u>Menu of the day</u>

Stiff papa

Worse

Beef gravy

On my way back, the love of my life was waiting for me, I went straight to him. We started digging into our food, I was a bit shy to eat in front of him and he was aware of that. "You don't have to be shy, I know you eat a lot" jokingly he told me. I had to laugh at him and told him I don't eat too much food. We were talking and eating, Tefo and i didn't have table manners, mostly him, and he was teasing me the whole time he told me that I was going to get fat if I continued eating. He made me laugh the whole time and I loved that he knew how to make me laugh, though sometimes he would tell me that I sometimes laughed for no reason. That I knew and was aware of, I was born like that I never got angry or ever be moody for no good reason.

I spent the whole weekend with tefo, I'd go in the morning and come back when the hostel was about to close, we did nothing but mostly laughing and kissing each other till we fall asleep."Its ok ill wait for you" he said to me. Tefo knew that I was still a virgin, he promised to wait till I was ready to have sex, I grew to love him even more each and every day. I used his phone to send please calls to my grandmother, Dibuseng was always not with me and she would call and not find me. Granny would call on Tefos phone and ask how I was; she would even speak to tefo too. She told me to wait till I finished school, she asked where Tefo was from and I told her all she needed to know.

"Someone wants to talk to you" Tefo told me. I knew from that moment that it was his mother, I was scared to speak to her and I asked Tefo to give me time and said I will speak to her someday. I was no longer scared to be seen with a boy mostly Tefo, everyone knew that we were dating, my grandmother knew that I was dating Tefo. She would send money to ShopRite and ask Tefo to accompany me to Setsing. The first time it wasn't easy, we had to go shopping together, I was embarrassed to put sanitary pads in the basket as he would hold it for me as I pick the things I wanted. I have to say that was embarrassing and sometimes I would ignore him and not take the sanitary pads and he would ask "di stay-free tsona?" I would shyly pretend as if I forgot about them, I had planned to buy them by the complex in the Pakistan shops even though I didn't like the brands they had I liked Kotex pads rather than stay free. Waking up next to Tefo was a dream come true, sometimes I would feel ready and would let him take my clothes off, he would kiss me everywhere, I would let him and say I am ready, but my uncle and Dave would come flashing in that moment, my dream to study in Cambridge would appear and there would be a baby crying for me. We both knew it was wrong, Tefo had dreams bigger dreams for the both of us and I too, we had to wait for the right moment we just had to. I loved to cuddle and mostly with him, he made cuddling fun and intimate. That night I dreamt of mom, she was with my dad, and we were playing on a green grass, though the dream was vivid. The sun was shining bright, the Dahlia flowers were beautiful and colourful. Mom and dad looked so happy; they were holding hands all the time. When the sun was setting mom changed into white clothes, she called us both from where she was standing, she was the most beautiful thing I've ever set my eyes on, they held hands with dad and I stood there between them, looking up their faces, the sun hurt my eyes and I closed my eyes, all of a sudden I couldn't see mom and dads face, I shook my head off, looking for their faces again I saw Tefo and myself, the little girl whom I thought was me was a beautiful little girl, who mostly had my moms face and my dad's nose. I woke up same time, I couldn't understand what was going on, no normal person can have such a dream unless they smoking weed and why was it so deceiving. I then went back to sleep,"Tefo bewitched me" I murmured, I then held my mouth with my hand and thanked God no one heard me.

Ausi Mathapelo was laughing out loud that morning, she was happy we couldn't understand why, when I went foward and handed my plate to her, she smiled and said, "Who is clever now". I knew what she was on about, us going home on weekends, she spoke as if she once told warned or she told us to stop the strike. Even if she did, we were never going to listen to her, they dilluted milk with water, they never fried the Vienna, the food they cooked was terrible and they would boil our chicken while they deep fried the ones they were going to eat.

September

It was few days before the Cultural day, I had never in my life celebrated Cultural day and had never taken it seriously not even from the school I come from, I always knew that it more than just about culture but braai day as we would call it. Ntate Mokeana had told us that he expected everyone to come with Traditional attires, he didn't care where you stay hostel or not he told me to go around the village to borrow the clothes. I needed something simple, something like Seshoeshoe and Seanamarena or Sefate or something as long as it was a blacket, and I knew who was going to help me out-Fedile.

I had to ask Fedile to help out, which she did but she was little bigger than me and her dresses were not going to fit. We had to run around the village looking for Seshoeshoe that was going to fit, I went to almost like five ladies my size before we found the right dress. The lady who was willing to borrow me the dress said it was dirty and it had to be washed first, she gave us a very strict instruction of how to wash it. I thought washing a Seshoeshoe was a piece of work and something to be done very quick, I was told to use cold water and mostly no washing machine which I was glad that we didn't have then she said no washing powder but sunlight washing bar. That day I was relieved that? I wasn't going to embarrass Ntate Mokeona, Our class had six if not nine certificates of participation hanging on the hall and had been coming first for Cultural presentations and attire. I had done all that had to be done with the dress and

Fedile had borrowed me her blanket 'Seanamarena', I was ready for the big day and I somehow couldn't wait. It was going to be my first time wearing my own Traditional representing a Mosotho woman, I was proud of being a mosostho though I never had to do all that had to be done by a Mosotho woman e;g like going to the mountains as my family does and I was allowed to. My uncle had mentioned it once and asked if I was interested and I said no, at that time I was still into Joburg life and never really had a chance to mingle and mix with my tribe, my friends were from different cultures and they too had their own mentality of town life and left the tradition mind somewhere I never knew.

The big day had arrived and I was wearing the clothes, together with the blanket, Fedile made sure that she came to the hostel before I left for school, I didn't know how to wear the blanket and I learned that ,wearing the Basotho blanket, you always have to make sure that the lines are horizontally and not vertically, she found me wearing it like that at first then she changed it for me, she even came with some make up to enhance my looks and I have to say she really did a good job in that. She was excited for me and had thought I looked beautiful, I didn't know that and I didn't think so, I felt older than I was, I felt more of an old woman than I looked. Everyone was cheering for me and said I looked beautiful, and some girls even said they couldn't wait for Tefo to see me. They started calling me Mme-Morema which is Tefos surname, I was smiling and couldn't stop, I haven't actually imagined me and Tefo Married, somehow I even thought we were going to be like malerato and

Mabekere, we looked like them sometimes long and short.

Everyone at school couldn't wait to see me; they were worried that I would come wearing normal clothes. They said I looked great. Almost all the girls were wearing the same blankets just different colours, some were wearing beads with their breast outside. It was quite a great experience for me as it was my first time seeing all the Basotho traditional clothes. Some I didn't know that they belonged to basothos. There was a long dress with lots of stripes that looked more like a Shibelani but it was long that I didn't know it was Basothos the list is endless...the whole day we didn't stay in class or did anything, we were preparing for the day and some were fixing each other and putting on makeup and some were practising their songs and dance routines. There were going to be different kinds of performances-singing, dancing and other Basotho things that i was to see for the first time. That day i was glad that my uncle had brought me to that school, it was more of knowing who my people are, going back to my roots sort of punishment, I was happy that I had come to qwa-qwa.

Tefo knocked at our window and he no longer came for Doobsie but I and i had to jump all the time, he gave me his phone and said my granny called and the phone died, he told me to keep it over night and charge it when electricity comes back. I was worried about his safety, i knew it wasn't safe and he had to travel to his place all alone, and I also heard that Phanga man escaped from prison, I took the phone and begged him to sleep at the hostel but he didn't answer me and just ran off. If something happened to Tefo I'd kill myself, it will break me and i didn't think i was going to be normal again. My love for tefo made the sun not to rise and both our love for each other made the sun to shine. Doobsie was no longer spending nights in our room, knor did she stay and chat with us as usual, I was worried about her more than I was worried about myself. I felt like I was a bad person, whatever punishment that awaited for me I was willing to take it, the last thing I wanted was people to be unhappy with me, and I didn't want Tefo and I to have enemies, not while we were still together. I believed love was a beautiful thing; people had to be happy when love was involved, and people had to smile and laugh, that was how I defined love.

When we woke up the lights were back and Mantahli had woke me to charge Tefos phone, I couldn't understand the urge on why would she wake me. I charged the phone and we waited impatiently for it to atleast pick up one bar or two, it later did and we brought it back to life. Tefos phone was a Samsung e250, white in colour and still brand new. The first thing i did was to send a call back to my grandmother; mantahli was jumping up and down begging me to open the pictures.

I needed to get Mantahli out of my way, and that was the only way how. We opened Tefos pictures and there he was, my prince charming, wearing that orange striped shirt of his I loved so much, I've always thought he looked hot in it. We scrolled and scrolled and only his pictures and friends were there, we had to go to another urban as we were both curious about it. There was a girl, I thought she was beautiful, she was chocolate in complexion, she had long natural relaxed hair, had the most beautiful eyes ever and her skin was beautiful. My heart started beating fast, it made more sound that the next person sitting next to me was able to hear it. My thumb was more curious than my thoughts or myself as it kept on scrolling, there were more pictures of that girl more than my pictures, I died a little and kept on rolling. There was another picture that captivated my eyes, I paused and stared at the picture more than ten minutes, I didn't even see when Mantahli left my side, and the girl was wearing the same school uniform the Sekgutlong uniform.

It didn't take me few minutes to put things together, I came to a conclusion Tefo was cheating on me, I thought my heart was going to stop beating, it felt like someone stabbed it, I felt cramps down my stomach. My body was shaking and thought I was going to get a fever at that very moment, if I had a dagger I would have stabbed my heart to stop beating. I didn't know what to do or how I felt, if that was how love was, I didn't want it. My mind told me to check the text messages and clarify the whole situation. Mantahli was back, sitting right next to me and waiting for me to say something but I didn't I couldn't. I went to the text messages, I fiddled with the phone as if it was mine and I knew it very well. I felt hopeless and worthless, I felt used, I felt small, and there was more than one text from the girl but plenty. At that same moment Mantahli told me she knew her and she always sees her with Tefo, I thought how I was going to see them I was stuck in Primary School the whole day. She told me her name was Nosisi, she explained the times they spend during break together, and Tefo always accompanying her to the taxi and that she doesn't stay around Mononthsa.

"Call her, call her, tell her she must leave Tefo alone" said Mantahli. I was frozen, I needed someone to come wake me up, I was having a horrible nightmare. I needed someone to bring cold water and wake me up, I couldn't wake up, no matter how many times I blinked I couldn't wake up. Kefilwe came in into our room followed by Mantoa aka Setswana, I don't remember when and how they got to me, they both were sitting next to me, together with Mantahli. I heard they were talking but i didn't hear what were they saying, i was trapped in a pit and couldn't find my way up.

i love you Nosisi

I love you too Tefo

i miss you

ill see you tomorrow at school

The texts were endless, I couldn't continue reading.

A few minutes later, I snapped out of it, it was not the end of the world and I had better things to live for. I came to Qwa-qwa to study and had to do that and leave, I didn't belong there and Tefo didn't belong to me either. My uncle was right, so was my grandmother. I had to remember to thank them when going back home. In fact, I would kiss them, I still had my virginity and I was going to save it to for the one I will marry right on the night of our honeymoon. I Automatically dialled Notices number, it rang and I couldn't wait to scream, I wanted her to feel the pain that I was feeling.She was dating Tefo,my superman,my life saver,my heart keeper, she had to feel her blood stop flowing through her veins.

"Hello"

"Hi...this is my boyfriends, I'm gonna ask you to stop calling him, stop sending these funny text messages, stop sending even please call me, you hear me?"

"All right ...alright"

"Oh and one more thing, once I see you with him I'll kill you, you hear me?"

I knew this was stupid, I am old enough now. I wasn't supposed to do that or to even call. I should have gone to Tefo actually, but hey...what was I going to do or say. **I WAS YOUNG STUPID AND INLOVE!**

I don't know how "all rights" may I heard from nosisi,she made me feel small and mostly stupid. I regretted calling her, deep down in my heart I knew I shouldn't have called her but it was my first time being cheated on, it was my first time finding myself in that kind of a situation."Poor girl, Palesa, how can you do such a thing. That poor girl is so quiet and innocent" said Mantahli."what?" that's all I said, she was the one who said I must call that poor girl, she was the one who even pushed me to open Tefos phone I wasn't prepared to, Mantahli made me do everything that destroyed my life forever.

What is love?

The day at school dragged and I wasn't prepared to go back to the hostel, I wanted nothing to do with him, not even his footprints. I looked so pale, hungry and I think I lost weight even worse. I couldn't get him out of my mind, the things he showed me, I never even knew that they existed. I never knew that a boy and a girl can cuddle, kiss, and say I love yours more than once. I never believed in fate but he made me to, we weren't even months old but countable weeks.

I found myself daydreaming and remember our happy moments, I've never thought me and Tefo could end up like this. I found myself smiling alone, there was a day when Tefo and were behind the classes, all the couples were there too. We were standing not far away from Makamane and Tlaleng, we heard a lot of laughter, people choking and some fell on the ground with laughter, we only saw Makamane and Tlaleng shaking themselves off, they had grass all over their clothes. Some girl came to our direction; she couldn't hold herself and was laughing the whole time. We asked what happened and she said, "Makamane was trying to be romantic by picking Tlaleng up and walking with her while in his arms and they both fell on the ground" we busted out with laughter and joined the other couples, I couldn't wait to tell my roommates. Those were my happy days and I was never going to experience them ever again.

I didn't want anyone near me, I hated everybody next to

me, Thato, Paseka and mostly I hated Abel with his wet nose. I hated everything, I hated the fact that he didn't want to explain, I hated myself because I didn't let him explain, he was going to lie to me. I hated that everyone in the hostel knew about it and they never told me, so it was obvious I was just something to pass his lonely time at the hostel with. I was still a stripper to him, I was still ngwana wako monontsha to him, I was nothing but a girl he wished to have sex with then dump after telling his friends at the hostel that he got me first.

I spent days with no food, I couldn't eat or laugh like before. My whole world was shut down, Tefo had let someone in our little bubble and it became overcrowded and it busted. I would get cold and there was nothing I used to do about it, my nightmares came back, and they got even worse. One of them was seeing my mom walking amongst a group of dead walking corpse, the people were too many to count, they were over a thousand, wearing black cloaks like those in a harry potter movie, this time she never looked at me no matter how many times I would call her name, she would continue to walk and I knew that I was never going to see her again. I went to maki, I needed answers from her and I needed them at that same moment. She said she doesn't want anything to do with my relationships, she told me Tefo loved me for real, but I also couldn't understand why he would have loved two people at once. She told me she knew as well, she said she didn't want to interfere; she said Tefo doesn't even spend much time with the girl but with me. I couldn't understand I needed someone to explain but there was no one there. I was scared to go to

Doobsie, she was going to say she told me or I thought I was clever.

The whole day at school I planned my life, I even drew it at the back of my books, and Tefo was not in it. I needed to show him that I was going to live without him, I was going to show him that he meant nothing, I've always considered myself an actress, I needed all those skills and I needed all of them to come to live. The bad thing was I didn't want to find a guy and play with his feelings, I didn't want some poor guys feelings to be broken just like I was. But I needed a guy to play boyfriend with; i didn't care if the boy would fall in love with me or not. I don't remember how i gave Tefo his phone, I've turned into a zombie all in the name of love; i even wondered that it wasn't loved but an infatuation. I've thought that love was stronger when two people having sex, i never had sex with him, but my love for him was that of a married woman whose husband filed for divorce while on honeymoon. My love for Tefo felt like an old RNB song, it was beautiful and true; it was too strong for me to deal with the loss.

Boyfriend number Two

Few weeks passed and I was recovering or maybe I thought I was, there was a boy who I thought was cute, his name was Fanyane. He was the cutest thing I've ever seen in a boy, I loved the way he dressed and the way he walked. I thought I was just crazy and my mind was playing tricks with me, the mistake I made was to make him notice me. Fanyane was tall, dark in but not too dark, he had Afro hair, very neat and was above my heart and I automatically thought that was just too cute. He was the shyest boy I've came across, he would let his friends speak on his behalf, and I would send the message to him as well. One day I got to meet him, he wanted to walk me to the hostel, he was quiet the whole time and didn't say anything. "You intimidate me" he told me. I knew that I did, I was strong and I knew it. I was still hurting and i talked too much. I prayed to God that i wasn't looking for Tefo in that poor boy's eyes, a few days later i found out that I was only into his height and mostly his sense of style, i kissed him once and all i wanted was to kiss Tefo and no one else.

Dimpho found out about me and Fanyane, everyone at school stopped calling me Stevovo but Fanyane. She told me of how Fanyane had never dated anyone in his life; she told me that he used to go to school with him and how he would be quiet. She was curious and asked if Fanyane talks and wanted to know what he normally talks about. I told her he does speak but not much, I told her that Fanyane is shy and didn't like me because I talk too much. My fling with him didn't last long and I was yet again single and was back to my old life and was moaning, moaning for someone who didn't even care about me and who didn't even bother to ask how I was holding up. The matrics were done writing their exams, I was also leaving school early, every day after writing, Mantahli and I would go to the complex and hang out, that was what everyone was doing. If you never went to the complex during exams then you would be left alone in the hostel like a moaning widow, I never wanted that, yes I was moaning but I needed to be around people.

Behind the jukebox building just next to the main road, I saw the Block bees, they were standing next to the poles and some were pinning themselves against them for balance. Mantahli asked me to come with her to see her friend Disebo, we didn't have a choice but to pass through the circle the boys had formed. They were busy talking about exams and to my surprise Tefo was one of the boys there, I felt my knees failing me, they turned yellow and I couldn't keep walking, I asked Mantahli to stand with me "I think I have a chewing gum under my shoe please stand with me" I said, I lied to Mantahli, I was losing my breath and I was glad she couldn't notice anything.

The girl who took my man

It took us ten minutes standing just not far from the boys, some loud light skinned girl came closer to the group of boys accompanied by another good looking girl whose face looked familiar. The light skinned girl greeted MAntahli and so did the dark one, she looked so shy she was even shy to say to say to MAntahli, her laughter was the only thing that I heard. My heart was dancing outside my chest, that was the only thing I heard. With a glimpse of an eye, the dark girl went to Tefo and pulled his arm and pulled him aside, Tefo was now standing with two of those girls.

a few minutes later the light skinned girl hugged the other girl, sure she was saying her goodbye then she turned away, the dark skinned girl was now alone with Tefo, I thought she didn't look scared to be standing with a boy in public with a lot of audience. "That's Nosisi, the girl you called, that's her right there with your ex-boyfriend" Said Mantahli. "huh?" I thought I didn't hear a thing, my ear felt like i was swimming in deep waters and the water was stuck in it, at some point I felt like i was near an ocean and all I could hear were small sea pebbles settling ashore and colliding with the sand. The message got to me late and it was already late because Mantahli never repeated herself.

I gained my consciousness, then the lightning stricken my Heart and I was no longer breathing like an asthma patient, but I was about to experience a heart attack. Tefo had guts to stand with that girl in front of me, mere fact was he saw me and he knew it was I, I didn't have a twin that he would have mistaken me for. "lets go, and we are going to pass right by them and we are going to say hi" I instructed Mantahli. That didn't happen at all, we just passed, I somehow thought of my reputation and how far I've become, I didn't want to be given onother name.

Passing through the couple was the most hardest thing to do, passing next to that grade twelve class was nothing, standing in front of the Monontsha assembly was nothing. The pain I felt was more than the pain Romeo felt when Juliet killed herself, in fact the pain of a gunshot wound was nothing compared to what I felt. The thing that killed me the most was that Tefo never said sorry, he never bothered to come and explain his faults he just kept quiet. To me it felt as if he never loved me at all, he lied to me all this while, he lied to his friends and to my grandma. When thinking about grandma, I died a little, she was going to call me, what would Tefo tell her? no old woman I cheated on your granddaughter, so we broke up? Or no I dumped her? I was confused.

On our way from Disebos house, Tefo and the girl were nowhere to be found. It killed me to think they went to his place; it killed me to think they might be having sex at that same moment. Somehow I even thought of asking someone to have sex with me, I needed all the pain the world was there to offer. I heard about the pain of first-time sex, and the blood that comes out. I needed someone to have sex with, I was going to ask that person to hurt me and give me pains with sleepless nights. Disebo and Mantahli were busy talking, laughing and looking at people, my body was there but my mind was in Tefo's room. I was glad even Disebo knew what I was going through, I didn't want her to think I was rude, she did ask me earlier on if I was ok and Mantahli was there to tell the story.

My baby is gone

The year was almost over, the grade Twelves had finished writing their exams, and some were leaving and some didn't. Somehow I pinched myself and prayed that Tefo will pass, I did hate him for hurting me but I wished him well. The hostel was empty and the matrics were gone, I thought they finished very early. Tefo never said anything, not even a goodbye, I didn't care; he was no longer mine but Nosisi. I also heard rumours that when the grade tens finished writing their exams, Nosisi was going to Lesotho to meet Tefos parents. If I didn't die that night then sure God was alive, I thought the girls were making things hard for me. They were actually trying to kill me, I didn't die physically but I was emotionally dead.

Every girl that was dating a grade twelve was moaning-Carly and Tlaleng were the worst; I even heard they cried when the brothers left. I didn't blame them I would have cried too, though I thought I've cried because of Tefo more than enough and had to stop the drama I mean life goes on. All the way to the dining hall and back everyone would hug the poor girls as if their boyfriends had died, Tlaleng told me that she had to call it off with Makamane, she said it was best if they did as they were never going to see each other again and i heard that Makamane cheated on her with Retshidisitswe Kefilwe's friend from school who was also staying at the animal farm.

My heart was broken and I didn't know if there was a chance to get something or someone to repair the pieces and put them back together again, I was stressed in a way that I even missed my periods. That was the most horrible and unpleasant moment of my life. What was funny was the fact that I thought I was pregnant; I know all girls used to be scared of that situation, but with me it was different, I was still a virgin. What my mother told me was that if I slept with boys my periods will stop that month and it would be possible that I could be pregnant.

I never understood anything about having sex, i thought that being closer to boys and cuddling was part of the whole process, I have to confess, my first kiss with Tefo was great though I was scared that he would make me pregnant with his saliva. It is crazy but this is something I don't believe that I did. If I had gone to Tefo and said I was pregnant he was going to think I have lost my mind. Yes I had lost everything and my mind was the last thing I wanted to lose.

I was alone in the room and I was desperate for my periods to come, yes they were painful but I wanted them I needed them to come. I kept on pressing my tummy, trying to feel if there was a baby in there or not. Somehow I didn't even have a clue of where the baby should be sitting inside the belly- all I knew was that babies sit in the belly-and that was it. The pressing made me sore and I was in pain, my belly button was the worst as I was pressing it the most. I stopped and prayed I don't know how many times and I thought God heard me and that he had to answer me by saying stop or enough, I wasn't ready to be a mother or to be the next black Merry mother of Jesus who fell pregnant without a man touching her. Hilarious!

Later that day I reminded myself that I had not spoken to Tumelo for the past eleven months, the last message I sent I had asked him to respond and he didn't, I had sent him a message telling him that I've kissed a boy and I like him, I asked him that we should remain childhood friends as I didn't want to cheat on my current boyfriend, I gave him reasons and that included us not being together and far away from each other. Of course that was before the lightning had stricken my thatch-roofed heart and burnt out.

My twelve-month diary was full, though I wasn't writing on it every day but all the important stuff were written in black and white, it was my therapy to write in it and it helped me a lot. I decided to read the diary and it lightened my mood at that very moment, I skipped some pages as I was not interested in some stories I wrote mostly of those that had Tefos name in them. I was also getting that each time I have to open my diary it was written...

p a l e s a

l o v e s

T e f o

1 2 2 3 2 2 1 1 1

2 3 3 5 2

4 8 3

78%

So I calculated that I loved Tefo loved 97%, those were the words that kept me going in life and reason why I always hoped to see onother day. The writing was not only in my diary but on my notebooks as well and I needed tips to cover up the writing as it was written in black and red ink.

I found something to laugh about and I had to call Mantahli and share it with her, so this other time Mantahi asked me if I wanted to be silly with her, that day I automatically agreed without knowing what was on her silly mind. She told me that she wanted us to go behind the classes and see what was going on, the point was to sneak on the couples, and see how they kiss well that was before I started dating and knew what was going on. She said we should walk behind the classes and pretend to be passing by or looking for some school project things, I thought the idea was awesome and it was going to be fun, we did go behind the classes and we saw Bongs and Sbabi kissing and we couldn't stop ourselves from laughing because Sbabi said to Bongs "wantoma Bongs", what made it funny was that her voice was so cute and small. Then our second couple was Mabekere and Malerato, the couple had always been funny and but they were just standing and talking, Mabekere always being the short one and MAlerato being the tall one. Those were the best days of my life and I am glad I kept a diary it helped a lot.

Life goes on

Grade nine exams were not bad at all, they weren't even exams but what they called CTA, sometimes we would even take the papers home to finish them off then bring them within the due date the teacher had requested. Thato and I had to do maths in class or go to Fedile's house for help, I was not good at all and I knew that, I think again it was just my negativity and my mindset I hated maths with every vein in my body. Ntate Lehodi once told us that " if you tell yourself that you dont like something that paticular thing wont like you either". I believed him and i always knew that he was a man of his words and what he said always stayed in my brain and i knew that I would use it somehow or somewhere needed.

The hostel was quiet and I couldn't wait to finish my exams so I can go home, all I hoped for was that I had passed and that I would take my report to David to see. I didn't want him to think I went to qwaqwa to waste his money, I had to give him hope and prove myself to him. I gained my consciousness and realised that I have been handling things the wrong way, I had let a boy destroy my life and mostly my future, he didn't care or to ask how was school and he didn't say sorry, I thought Tefo was just sent by Satan to destroy my life. Yet again I was thankful that he was part of my life, I didn't know anything about boys and he introduced me to that world. Tefo was a reason and a lesson both at the same time, never to trust a boy ever in your life and dont ever show him that you love him my uncle was right! I missed home, I missed my granny and mostly my brother Thato, and I missed my lonely life.

How we broke up- told by Tefo

It was his birthday, 30th August, just a few weeks after mines. Everyone was at the complex as usual, though it was a Thursday-the boy were drinking, celebrating my boyfriends birthday, he was turning eighteen. I was at the hostel in my room as always, I wished to be there with him, I wished to sit right next to him. I never liked him when he was drunk though he was funny, but he was fragile, he was vulnerable and needed my protection, I never imagined him falling as that would tear me into pieces.

A few minutes later some girls from the hostel came to my room; they were running and not walking like normal people. "What is wrong guys, why you not knocking?" I questioned them.They didn't answer. The girls were still in their uniform, I was already changed into my pyjamas. They were breathing heavily like they were being chased by someone who was going to kill or rob them and some were even losing their breaths. I wished they could breathe, I knew they had something important to say, and sure it was about me or someone I cared for deeply. It then hit me "Didi something happens to Tefo? Toka? Tshepang? What?"

One of them sat on my bed and started spilling the beans, my mind stopped functioning at that very moment, I was able to hear echoes but didn't hear what exactly were they talking about. All I heard was that Tefo my own Tefo, my one and Only Tefo was with that girl Nosisi. The girls told me that they were very cosy and looked more than just cozy, they told me that they walked to Tefos place together holding hands.

I didn't want to hear any more so did I want to hear his name, I snapped and told them to leave my room at once, what broke my heart the most was that Mantahli was one of the witnesses. How could he? How could he do that in front of my own roommate? It was quite obvious he wanted her to see them, it broke my heart to know that everyone from the hostel was there, not just my roommate. I knew they were classmates and all that, but I was her roommate, I thought she was more than that to me, a friend-someone I could trust with my life, I was wrong about Mantahli she has never been there for me.

The speed and time I took from changing from pyjamas were unpredictable, no one could have majored that not even Albert Einstein, what was on my mind was to catch him red handed, I wanted him to see me, I wanted him to choose who he wanted to be with. Some group of girls were behind me, they saw that I was ready for a fight, I didn't know myself if was going there to fight or not. I was travelling at the speed of sound, I dont remember how many steps I took within a second.

The complex was packed, students in brown khaki uniforms scattered everywhere like soldiers preparing for war, i looked from every corner and my boyfriend was nowhere to be found, i couldn't locate him anywhere, I couldn't even smell his scent. I knew that he was never in his uniform, I had to ask around and

I knew who to ask, I went straight to Dlomo-that guy knew everything and I knew he were to crack the shit out of his lungs with laughter. I was upset and I needed answers and my so called boyfriend was the one to answer all that I wanted to know.

With the blink of an eye, he walked out of Kwa mavundla carrying bottles of Smirnoff Storm; he was just the sexiest thing in my life. He was wearing a white top with a hoodie that I loved so much, matching white all stars boot and black Levis jeans. He looked so amazing and I couldn't believe that i was to start a fight with him; I loved him so so very much. I went straight to him and the first thing he said was "stripper oso matha di complex le wena" he saw I was angry and he saw the crowd was beginning to pay attention to our direction, I couldn't care less about the crowd or whoever that was there, I didn't even see anyone with me but him, it has always been like that angry or not, we have been working on tightening our own little bubble to be stronger and it worked effectively. He once told me that there should never be anyone in our relationship but the two of us, and that was how our bubble was tightened; it was built on trust and friendship.

"Oh God se ba ojwetsitse?" meaning they have told you. All I asked him was who and what was he talking about. Tefo was my first kiss and my one and only boyfriend that I called a boyfriend for real, whatever he told me I believed him and that was how i was, he told me quite a lot of things and said that girl was nothing but was just talking to her as she was dating one of his friends and he had to talk to her since the friend and the girl were no longer talking to each other blah blah blah.

He told me this and said "that's what happened"...maybe he doesn't know that he had hurt me more than twice but that's a story for another day. We all get hurt and we all fight with the people we love.

My goals in 2008...
Break my virginity, and break more of my virginity!

Lord knows that I loved Tefo and I still love him even today, he was the reason why he had made us an item and again it was his doing that I found Tefo attractive, God knows that I still love him even though he broke my heart. If I had to be with another boy, I'd kill myself, if I have to marry someone else I'd say I was bewitched. If I didn't get to spend the rest of my life with tefo then God please take me and kill me as I would have already been dead anyway.

2008

I spent the whole December holidays in Johannesburg, I made a promise to myself not to go to Matatiele during any given holiday or I'd look like a farm girl who plays hide and sick with pigs and goats-hahaha just like those pigs my grandad ntate Koali had when I was young, I spent my whole life running after those pigs when they got a chance to escape, the little ones were the hardest to capture. I couldn't wait to go back to qwaqwa, I felt a little older too though I knew that I didn't have an ID but I was turning seventeen in August I couldn't wait, and all my wishes came true, that includes kissing a boy before my 18th birthday though I was still a virgin, I couldn't wait to see if my grandmother was finally going to talk boys with me, for crying out loud she never talked periods and pregnancy either, well simply because I never gave her a chance to do so. The day I got my periods I just kept quiet and went straight to her and said "can I have money for pads please" that's all I said and she wasn't shocked or anything she just said, "oh you've started?" And I said yes then went straight to her purse and took a R10 and went straight to the shops and came with penty liners. When I think of that I laugh all the time, when I came back she asked when did I start and how did it happen and asked if it wasn't sore all I said was "I learned everything in my Life Orientation class, so I know everything, so lets not talk about it" I really didn't want to talk about it as it was embarrassing back then plus my brother Thato was sitting next to her watching TV, mostly telling her all that was going to be hard for me so I brushed the topic out of the way and carried on with my life and the penty liners I were to use for my heavy periods.

I had passed my grade nine and was finally going to boarding school yet again, but was excited that i was going to change uniforms and most of all i was going to be a high school student. My granny was so happy and i was glad that i made her proud, i was happy that i was yet again going to go to qwaqwa and prove to David that his money was not being wasted. I was also happy that i was going to stay with Mrs Motaung my Primary school principal, she had asked David and Granny if she can take me on weekends, and they said yes with their smiles just above their ears, all they cared for was that she was a principal, a woman and of course older and was to be a good example in my life. I also knew that if I needed help with school work she was to be there to the rescue though everyone who knew me were to be shocked but I didn't care.

Only a few days were left till I head back to hell again, I have to confess that I couldn't wait. I was prepared and I wasn't new and I knew what was to happen at the hostel. What warmed my heart the most was the fact that I was, of course, to be early than last year, I had asked my granny to prepare all my school things and was happy that she bought me new bedding and it was blue and bright. The bedding that I had last year was too brown like a boy's one, my granny said I deserved it and it was to be easy to wash. Apart from being easy to wash, I've never been tidy in my life, my mom and I were not good friends in that department, we used to fight a lot and she would shout at me to the point where she would end up being diagnosed with laryngitis. My mom was loud!

Staying with Mantahli yet again was the last thing I needed, I didn't want her mood swings to ruin my life, I had to make sure that I study and always remain calm and stress-free. I was of course still confused about the subjects i was to choose in high school, I didn't want to do something hard to solve and definitely, maths was the least of them.

Coming to think of the subjects to choose I didn't really know, ever since i was young I've never dreamt of being anything fancy in life though having money and being filthy rich had always been my priority. I didn't know how I was going to make money but it had always been my dream to have it, and that was the beginning of shaping my future; hold on a minute uhmmmm I've always wanted to travel the world, be a writer and look pretty and fashionable all the time. Lesly Pearse and Virginia Andrews are my favourite writers and that includes my best of best Jan van de fruit, these writers inspire me and I've always wanted to be just like them and be a successful author.

I had to make myself a favour and again to please my family and not forgetting David, he was yet again going to pay for my fees till i finish my matric. I am forever indebted to him and i had to make sure that i had to show gratitude by giving out the best results all the time, and i knew exactly how to do that.

Rules for the new year

- No boys a big no!
- No friends
- No partying even though others were to do so
- No alcohol
- No lazing around
- Become the best you can be
- Pay attention all the time
- Love your Books
- No procrastinating
- No Mantahli (she's moody)
- Always do your homework
- Study every day ... from January till December no breaks

These were the things to get me through the year, and I knew they were going to work if I had to stick to them.

THE END OF BOOK ONE...

Ok so I had a phone; Motorola Razer, I felt like a complete 100% teenager, my life was complete all wrapped into one. I had a collection of my rock music, Maroon 5, Coldplay and the script without forgetting the Kings of Leon. My screen saver had my granny's picture sitting on the bed, I had mxit, and atleast ten numbers of my family and two of which were that of December and my best friend Sindy-without forgetting my best friend in a cousin Tunkie, I knew her moms number by head and didn't save them